KU-785-220

PREY

My fight to survive the Halifax grooming gang

CASSIE PIKE
with Katy Weitz

JOHN BLAKE

Published by John Blake Publishing,
The Plaza,
535 Kings Road,
Chelsea Harbour,
London SW10 0SZ

www.johnblakebooks.com

www.facebook.com/johnblakebooks
twitter.com/jblakebooks

First published in paperback in 2019

PB ISBN: 978 1 78946 084 1
Ebook ISBN: 978 1 78946 098 8

All rights reserved. No part of this publication may be reproduced, stored in a retrieval
system, or transmitted in any form or by any means, without the prior permission in
writing of the publisher, nor be otherwise circulated in any form of binding or cover
other than that in which it is published and without a similar condition including this
condition being imposed on the subsequent purchaser.

British Library Cataloguing-in-Publication Data:
A catalogue record for this book is available from the British Library.

Design by www.envydesign.co.uk

Printed and bound in Great Britain by Clays Ltd, Elcograf S p. A

1 3 5 7 9 10 8 6 4 2

© Text copyright Cassie Pike and Katy Weitz 2019

The right of Cassie Pike and Katy Weitz to be identified as the authors of this work has
been asserted by them in accordance with the Copyright, Designs and Patents Act 1988.

MIX
Paper from
responsible sources
FSC
www.fsc.org   FSC® C018072

Every reasonable effort has been made to trace copyright-holders of material
reproduced in this book, but if any have been inadvertently overlooked the publishers
would be glad to hear from them.

Some names and identifying characteristics mentioned in this book have been changed
in order to protect the privacy of certain individuals.

John Blake Publishing is an imprint of Bonnier Books UK Ltd
www.bonnierbooks.co.uk

This book is dedicated to all survivors –
past, present and future

Falkirk Community Trust	
30124 03118398 3	
Askews & Holts	
B PIK	£8.99
MK	

FALKIRK COMMUNITY TRUST

30124 03118398 3

CANCELLED

PREY

Contents

PART 2 – AFTER

Prologue

22 July 2011

Keep it together. Keep it together, Cassie.

I breathed heavily. Sitting in the backseat of the police car, I felt the panic beginning to rise in my chest. We passed the turning for Manchester ages ago, and I thought that's where Pete and June were taking me.

'So, are we not stopping here?' I asked, as we whizzed past the turn-off from the motorway.

'No,' Pete said gently. 'Not here. Just relax, Cassie. It's going to be a long drive.'

I let the gentle hum of the car soothe me and, exhausted, I dozed off. I woke with a start a while later. The landscape passing by the window looked different somehow: more cows and countryside, not so many buildings.

Where are we going? I had no idea, and some part of me didn't want to know. I just wanted to get far away from it all; far away from the horrible life I'd been living for far too long.

My phone buzzed insistently in my pocket. It had been ringing non-stop since we left Halifax, though I didn't recognise any of the numbers.

Now a text pinged into my inbox: 'Hiya sexy – are you coming out?'

And then another: 'Cassie – wanna come for a chill?'

I sighed and put my phone back in my pocket. *I don't want to take their calls any more, don't want to answer their texts. I want nothing more to do with any of them.* I lay my hand on the carrier bags next to me. Inside, two empty vodka bottles clinked together. I peered into the bag and was relieved to find a third was still half full. *At least I can have a drink soon.*

The booze was left over from my sixteenth birthday the day before. I hadn't done much for the occasion – just went to the park and bought something to drink. Some of the men turned up and drank with me. The best thing was when Social Services arrived with money to buy new clothes. We went to New Look and I got a few new tops and leggings. It was a relief because, for the past few years, all I'd had to wear were hand-me-downs from my sisters. If I wanted anything new, I had to steal it.

Afterwards, I had a little money left over so I got a spray tan. It felt nice to be given a treat, even if it was by Social Services. It was more than my dad had ever given me. The last time he had remembered my birthday, he'd given me a blank card to fill in myself!

It was all over now with my dad. There was no going back.

He didn't want me at home any more; in fact, he didn't want me anywhere near him. I had asked to go back to visit the family but he told me no. And the one time I turned up near his house, he whacked me over the head. For the past few weeks I had been living at the foster carers and hadn't seen any of my family. I hadn't even been at the foster carers all that much, though – the pick-ups had become so frequent that I barely spent any time in the house at all. The guys would come by, put me in a car and take me away for the night, or longer. Sometimes I would disappear for days at a time. The booze and all the drugs wiped me out for hours and I would wake up a couple of days later, God knows where, with my clothes around my ankles. Sometimes they took me back to Halifax, sometimes I'd have to get back on my own. And the foster carers couldn't do a thing about it. They seemed like nice people but they were clueless. And I was homesick. All I wanted was to pop into my dad's place for a cup of tea and a chat – maybe catch up with my sister Tammy. But it all went very wrong.

I had bumped into Dad outside Betfred, which was near the house, and just the sight of me seemed to make him mad.

'What do you think you're doing here?' he shouted at me on the street, his face contorted in rage. He didn't care who was listening. 'What the fuck are you doing here, Caz?'

He didn't wait for a reply, just rolled up the *Racing Post* and started whacking me on the head with it. The blows themselves didn't hurt as much as his words.

'Go away, Caz! Go on, get lost. We're sick of you. Sick of it all and you're not welcome back.'

'Dad, please . . . please . . . will you just let me come to the house?'

'NO!' he roared. 'You've fucked it all up. Look what you've done. You've destroyed the family. It's all your fault, the whole situation. You're not welcome at the house any more.'

I started to cry.

'Look at the state of you,' he spat, disgusted. 'Look at you – you're an embarrassment.'

I hardly knew what I looked like any more. When did I last change? I couldn't remember. I pulled my blouse down and hitched up my jeans. They were only a size 6 but they were falling off me. I knew I was too thin, but there didn't seem to be much time in my life to eat, and I wasn't hungry in any case. Anyway, what did it matter what I looked like? All I wanted was to be with my family. I started to sob.

'Please, Dad,' I repeated. 'I'm sorry. I won't stay long, I promise. Just let me home for a brew.'

'Everyone's had enough. Everyone's broken because of the situation. You broke the family. Now fuck off.'

I walked away, crying, and in that moment I knew I could never go back again. It was over. He'd made it clear they never wanted me back. And I didn't blame him. I mean, all of this, it was my fault, wasn't it? All the bad choices I'd made over the years had brought me to this point. Every time I'd got drunk, got high, got in a stranger's car – it was all my own stupid fault. It was almost a relief when the next guy pulled up alongside me on the street and told me to get in. At least he would have some gear, maybe some fet, a few pills. I would soon be able to forget about it all; forget

about Dad and the humiliating encounter on the street. I didn't
care any more. I just didn't care . . .

So when the two police officers arrived at the foster carers'
house the day after my sixteenth birthday, I knew I had no
choice but to go with them. After all, I didn't have anywhere else
to go now my family didn't want anything to do with me, and
maybe, just maybe, they could take me somewhere far enough
away that the men couldn't find me any more. Pete, one of the
officers, spoke kindly to me, the way he always had.

'Just pack your things, Cassie, and we'll be on our way.'

'Where are we going?' I asked for the tenth time that morning.

'You'll find out soon enough, don't worry.'

I scrabbled around to find my possessions. There wasn't much.
Everything I owned fitted into two black bin liners: some clothes,
my hair straighteners, toiletries and the booze. All the while I
thought about my dad and my sisters – I wondered if I would
ever see them again. Now, with the miles of road disappearing
behind us, I was further from home than I had ever been in
my life. I was dying for a fag but Pete refused to stop. The sun
hung low in the sky and I wondered if we would be driving
through the night.

'Are you going to tell me where we're going?' I asked Pete.

This time he sighed. 'I've told you, Cassie, you're going to a
new foster family and we have very good reasons to be taking you
so far from Halifax. But we'll be there soon. It's not long now, I
promise. They're really nice people and they've got two daughters
close to you in age. It's going to be different now. It's a fresh start
for you.' He smiled at me in the rear-view mirror.

A fresh start . . . yes, that's what I need. I briefly caught sight of my reflection – a black eye, smudged mascara and fake tan streaks around my neck. It had been going on for too long now. *I'm so tired, so very tired of it all. I want a fresh start. A new life. A second chance. I just want it all to stop.*

PART 1

BEFORE

'You cannot swim for new horizons until you
have courage to lose sight of the shore.'
WILLIAM FAULKNER

1.

Ali

'HEY! HOW YOU DOING?'

The guy who pulled up in the car next to me was Asian, probably in his mid-twenties. I had just got off the bus from school and was walking home, swinging my bag by my side. I didn't recognise him at all.

'Do I know you?' I asked.

'Not really,' he said, smiling, taking a pull on a cigarette. 'My name is Ali. I saw you outside Simone's house the other night. I think you were there for a party. I live in the house opposite. I saw you having a fag in the garden. You're really pretty.'

'Oh, thanks.' I smiled, feeling my cheeks grow hot. But I kept walking while his car crawled along slowly next to the pavement.

'Hey, listen, do you want to go for a drive and a bit of a smoke later?'

I stopped for a second and thought about what was waiting for me at home. 'Yeah, why not,' I said, shrugging.

What's your name?'

'It's Cassie,' I said, tugging at the skirt of my school uniform, suddenly a little self-conscious.

'Well, Cassie, why don't you give me your number and I'll message you later? We'll go for a drive, have a drink and a chill somewhere.'

'Yeah, that sounds good,' I said. So I gave Ali my number and he drove off.

He had noticed me . . . he said I was pretty. It's nice to be told that sort of thing, especially by an older guy.

By now, I was just a couple of minutes from home. I turned the corner of Queen's Road and hurried towards our small close behind the main road. Our three-bedroom semi sat at the end of a quiet street in the east end of Halifax, a part of the city filled with people from many different backgrounds and countries, like Pakistan, Bangladesh and Poland. In my primary school I had been one of only two white kids in my whole year and there were just four white children in the whole school. It wouldn't have bothered me except the Pakistani children didn't talk to me – they spoke to each other in their own language, and when they did talk to me it was to call me names like 'white bitch'. At first I would tell the teachers but it didn't seem to make much difference so I just put up with it. That was why I had chosen a secondary school over four miles away from home, and the reason I had to catch a bus there every day – I wanted to make some new friends. I just hoped it was Tammy watching Mum today and not Dad. I wasn't in the mood to face Dad.

'I'm home,' I yelled, as I let myself in through the front door. I hung up my bag and coat on the peg in the hallway and walked into the lounge to find Mum in her usual place in front of the TV. It was a relief to see she looked okay – clean and tidy and not upset. That meant Dad was out.

'Alright, Mum?' I kissed her on the forehead and grabbed the cold mugs of tea from the table next to her. Mum nodded, though not in a way that most people would recognise. Her blonde head bobbed and jigged about in funny directions but her eyes told me all I needed to know. She was fine.

'T-t-tea?' she asked.

'Yeah,' I laughed. 'Give me a minute, Mum. I've only just got back from school. Look, I'll put the kettle on, alright?'

Mum nodded again then went back to watching *Hollyoaks*, one of her favourite soaps. It was nice to have her home again for a few days. She was in respite care most of the time now, which was good in some ways because I didn't have to worry about her being at home alone, though I did miss having her there. The place felt very empty without her. Now I fussed around her, picking up abandoned plates of toast and adjusting the blanket on her knees. I sniffed the air. It was probably time to change her nappy too, though I wasn't sure I had the strength to lift her on my own. Maybe Tammy could help, if she was around.

Mum looked at me, let out a little noise and I grinned back. I knew she was happy to see me. We had a special bond, the two of us, and I liked it when she came home. Poor Mum. She had been diagnosed with Huntington's disease when I was just a year old and she was thirty-one. Since then she had been in a steady decline. It's a cruel disease, Huntington's, gradually robbing you of your movement and speech over a number of years, replacing them with involuntary spasms and incomprehensible sounds and grunts. Mum knew what was coming because it's an inherited disease; she'd watched her own mother and two older sisters go through it before her. At first she'd tried to carry on as normal but she kept falling over. In the beginning, she had used sticks to get around and, this way, she would try to walk me to school. The other schoolkids weren't very nice about her – they said she grunted like a pig and made mocking piggy sounds whenever they saw her. It upset me but there wasn't much I could do about it. They didn't understand that she was ill.

The sticks only worked for a short time and then she got a walking frame to help her get about, but she kept tripping up over the wheels. Eventually Dad said it wasn't a good idea for her to take me to school any more in case she had a serious accident. He cared about her in his own way, I suppose. And I would worry too – she would drop me off at the gates of my primary school, the bell would ring and then I'd have to go into lessons but all I could think about was whether Mum had got home okay. If she fell in the street, would somebody help her? Or if she fell at home, would someone be there to look after her? It happened so often that I felt constantly anxious in school.

Fortunately my two sisters were often home to help her – Marie was eleven years older than me, and Tammy was eight years older. We would do the things for Mum that she couldn't do for herself any more, like put on her moisturiser – she got through tubs of Nivea Creme like there was no tomorrow – apply her make-up, brush her hair and do her nails. She liked to look her best, that's for sure. In fact, when she was a young woman, she was gorgeous – tall and slim with short blonde hair, blue-green eyes and a dazzling smile. I've seen the pictures of her on holiday with her friends, singing karaoke, having a drink and a good time, living it up. She was bubbly and outgoing, my mum, and everyone said she was stunning. But the disease, it takes away all your movements and leaves you with these unexpected jerks and twisting motions, so by the time I was growing up she could no longer even hold an eyeliner pencil or apply lipstick without getting it everywhere. Even Dad had to shave her armpits, and he would make us all swear not to tell anyone.

'She likes it a certain way,' he'd whisper conspiratorially, his eyebrows waggling up and down. This was funny to us as young kids, and we would crack up.

When I was five, Marie had her little girl, Dara, and they moved into their own place, so then it was just me, Tammy and Dad at home. Dad did his bit, I suppose. We all did, taking it in turns looking after Mum. In the last couple of years, before she moved into the respite home, it was more than just putting on her make-up – we had to dress her, take her to the toilet and feed her. When it became impossible to keep lifting her to the upstairs toilet, she started wearing adult nappies and then we had to change them. It wasn't always easy, especially if there was no one around to help. My primary school teachers told me off for being late most mornings, but no matter how hard I tried to be on time there was always too much to do before I could leave the house. They said I should set off earlier but I had to get Mum dressed, fed and changed before I could even think about getting myself ready. Dad didn't help me. He wasn't what

I would call a 'hands-on parent'. In fact, he wasn't around much at all.

From as far back as I can remember my dad was always in and out. He would get up in the morning, drink the tea I'd made him and then go out for the day – to the pub or the bookies, placing bets on the horses, the dogs, football or whatever took his fancy. I rarely saw him and, when he was at home, he was either high or drunk or both. The rare times he was at home he usually had the TV on, tuned to the horse racing, and he'd sit in front of that all day, a can of lager in one hand and a fag in another. If he was in a good mood, he'd ask me which horse I fancied and he'd put a bet on for me. He often had his friends round and they'd all smoke and drink together. So it was up to me and my sisters if we wanted our clothes washed or a hot meal made. I learned pretty quickly how to take care of myself. We never went out together as a family, except to accompany Dad to the bookies. I must have been pretty young the first time we did that. I clung to my mum's arm, under strict instructions to hold onto her wheelchair, while Dad pushed her the short distance to the door of Betfred and then left us outside while he went in to place his bets. Mum and I waited for ages before he came back out again.

I don't think she minded too much. At least it was a bit of a change for her. After she stopped walking me to school, she didn't get out of the house much. She had a routine and we all had to stick to it rigidly. She'd have a cigarette, then a cup of tea – milk, two sugars – and then we'd take her to the toilet. That was it, every day, every twenty minutes – fag, tea, toilet. It was quite demanding because we'd frequently run out of things like milk or sugar, and then I'd have to go and knock on the neighbours' doors to borrow some. I didn't have any money myself and Dad was never around to ask, so I relied on the goodwill of those around us when I was stuck without Mum's essentials. Because if Mum didn't get her fag, tea and toilet, then she'd start to shout, and I found that really upsetting.

But the worst thing was when Dad got angry. 'What do you think you're doing, you stupid bitch?' I'd hear him shout from the upstairs loo, and my blood would run cold. I knew, I just knew she'd missed the seat or done something by accident like peeing on the floor and he would be going mad at her.

'YOU FUCKING STUPID BITCH!'

Then there would be a sound like a smack, and the next thing I'd hear was my mum whimpering and crying. I'd race upstairs to see him standing over her, his hand raised again as if he was going to whack her, and I'd do my best to try to stop him.

'Dad, please stop!' I'd beg. 'It's not her fault. Leave her alone.'

Sometimes it would work and I'd manage to calm him down enough that he would walk away and leave her alone. But more often than not he would just carry on.

'Get out, Caz, this is none of your fucking business,' he'd growl, and I knew not to push him too far. It wasn't just me – we all tried to stop Dad from hitting Mum – but then he would turn on one of us and he often ended up hitting Tammy and then telling her to clean up the mess afterwards.

I wish I could say it was once in a blue moon, or once in a while, but it wasn't. It happened a lot more than that – three, four times a week maybe, and it was always the same. Mum would have a little accident that wasn't her fault, like spilling her drink, and Dad would fly off the handle, hit her and shout nasty things at her. It was frightening when he lost it because he seemed so out of control. I think that was the drugs. When the red mist came down he transformed into a completely different person. He'd pin her down, sit on top of her and bawl in her face: 'I WISH YOU WERE DEAD, YOU BITCH! I FUCKING HATE YOU. WHY DON'T YOU JUST DO US ALL A FAVOUR AND FUCKING DIE, YOU STUPID FUCKING COW.'

And she would lie there, unable to move or speak or do anything to defend herself. She was helpless. On and on he'd go, shouting at her, and it looked like he wouldn't stop until he did something really awful to her. But eventually it would all die down and he'd get up and walk out of the house, slamming doors as he went.

The thing is, he was always sorry afterwards. He would cry and apologise and tell Mum that he didn't really mean it and he just got frustrated or overwhelmed sometimes. And I think she forgave him a lot because, well, she didn't really have any choice, did she? If he didn't take care of her, who would? I mean, she had us but we were still children. Afterwards I'd go up to Mum and we would both cry together.

'Don't worry about Dad,' I'd whisper. 'Just ignore him. He doesn't mean any of that stuff.'

'I'm fine,' she'd sniff, trying not to let her emotions show. 'It's just . . . just dust in my eye.' But I knew it wasn't dust. How could he say those things to her? It just wasn't fair.

By the time I was witnessing all this, Mum didn't have anyone else in her life but us. Her mother and older sisters had all developed the illness and died young. She had one brother who was still alive but we only ever saw him at Christmas. The friends she'd made as a young woman all disappeared until she was left alone in the house with no visitors. The only people she saw were the health professionals and a mobile hairdresser who came once a month. If Dad's side of the family came to visit they never stayed long and Dad always made it seem like everything was fine. He never asked anyone for help or to spend time with her. So she was alone most of the time, and I think if it wasn't for us she would have been very lonely.

Then, when I was nine years old, Social Services assessed Mum's needs and said it was time for her to go into respite care. It was a big relief to me because it had become so hard to care for her, as Marie had moved out some time ago, so it was just me and Tammy. And Dad didn't like Social Services much, so we never asked for their help. He told us we weren't to talk to them about anything that was going on in our house.

'Don't tell them fuckers anything, right? he'd say. 'You can't trust 'em. Don't talk to them, Caz. Don't tell them about the weed I'm growing. Or how I hit your mum, or about anything else that goes on here, right? Or there'll be hell to pay.'

I knew exactly what he meant – if Dad thought I'd ratted on him, he would have given me a hiding for it. So when the social workers visited I was careful not to say anything that would make him look bad. Mum went into the care home and, from that point on, Dad spent more and more time out of the house. There were some weeks I didn't see him for days at a time, and if we ran out of food or the heating went off, well, there wasn't much I could do about it. Sometimes Tammy would have enough money to put the heating back on, or to go down the corner shop for bread and cheese to make sandwiches. But if there was no food in the house and I didn't have any money I'd have to nick something to eat: a packet of crisps, some sweets or a can of pop.

With Mum in the care home most of the week there didn't seem much point going home any more, so I spent a lot of time at Marie's place, helping her out with her daughter Dara, and in the evenings I'd hang around the People's Park with my friends, which was a ten-minute walk from her house. If the weather was nice we'd sit on the gently sloping hill that led from the pavilion at the top down towards the duck-filled ponds at the bottom. Or, if it was raining, we'd all huddle under the large bandstand and share fags. One night, at the all-night garage round the corner from Marie's place, I met a girl called Simone. Marie would send me out there late at night to get baby formula, fags or snacks for the kids. Simone was often there too and we got talking – she was a couple of years older than me, at thirteen, but she seemed really nice and we got on well. Her home life wasn't easy either – her mum was very fat and sofa-bound. It meant Simone had to care for her and also her little brother, who had learning difficulties.

Simone was something of a kindred spirit. Life at home wasn't great for either of us, so we liked to go out to relax and get away from the stress. She introduced me to some other friends of hers and we'd all meet at the park to hang out, listen to music, drink vodka and smoke weed. Occasionally I would steal a cannabis plant from my dad's collection, or take one of his bongs, and we'd all get high together, giggling like maniacs.

It was a cool September evening, a couple of weeks after I had started at my new secondary school, when Simone had a party in her back garden. And that's where Ali had said he'd seen me. So, after spotting me in the street and getting my number, Ali picked me up and we drove to a car park on the edge of town where he rolled a joint and we had a smoke and a chat. He seemed really friendly and we spent a couple of hours sitting there, just chatting. He told me he was married and had two kids. Then he pulled out a bottle of vodka and we shared that. I told him how I was helping my sister with her little girl and he talked to me about his kids. He dropped me back home later that evening and I didn't think anything more of it. A couple of days later I got a message on my phone from a number I didn't recognise.

'Hi Cassie – u okay? Fancy coming out 4 a chill tonight?'

I looked at the number, a little confused. 'Yeah, alright,' I messaged back. 'Who r u?'

'My name is Imie. I know your sister from school.'

'How did u get my number?'

'From Ali. Fancy coming out?'

I was eleven years old and that was how it started.

2.

Imie 1 & Imie 2

TAMMY AND I WERE on our way to Asda when the car pulled up next to us.

'Hey, Tammy, you alright? What have you been up to all these years?'

My sister squinted at the bloke in the car – he was Asian, with a small goatee, and he looked around twenty-five, maybe older. She took a few seconds to recognise the face.

'Oh, alright,' she replied. 'Weren't we at school together?'

'Yeah, that's right. Who's this, then, your little sister?'

'Yeah, this is Cassie.'

'Hiya,' I said.

'Cassie, yeah? We've been texting. It's Imie, remember?'

'Oh yeah . . . you alright?'

'How old are you, Cassie?'

'Twelve.'

'Wanna go for a drive? Have a smoke? Chill?'

'Yeah,' I said, shrugging. 'Why not?'

'Great. I'll pick you up later.'

Tammy and I got the shopping, hunting down the best deals we could find, managing as best we could on the fifteen pounds Dad had given us that morning.

'How are we meant to do a proper shop for fifteen quid?' Tammy asked Dad, exasperated, after he'd reluctantly handed over the cash. It had taken a whole hour of badgering just to get that money and she looked at the three fivers in her hand with a sort of tired anger. 'How is this meant to buy all our shopping? There's nothing in the house!' she went on. 'We need toilet paper, washing powder, food, tea, milk, bread, beans, bleach . . .'

'That's plenty,' he said, waving her away. 'You can get all that for a tenner, let alone fifteen! You just want more money for yourself. You're all bleeding me for cash to buy fags and booze, I know. Buy your own fucking fags! Don't fuck with me, Tam.'

'Oh, for Christ's sake, Dad!' Tammy turned away in disgust. We both knew she would have to fork out money herself if we wanted to get everything on the list. It was just as well Tammy had a couple of jobs. She worked nights in the pub up the road and during the day she had a packing job in a factory, so she usually had some spare cash on her. Dad never gave us enough money for the shopping and always gave us real earful if we asked for more.

I didn't bother with breakfast for myself any more – I could usually manage on one meal a day and a few snacks. If I wanted a smoke, I'd go to the park and find someone who had some weed. At least the heating was on.

Later that evening Imie texted me, so I went out to meet him in his car. He had rolled a joint and we smoked it together. Then he said, 'Hey, my cousin's house is down the road. He's away at the moment so I'm house-sitting for him. Wanna go there?'

'Sure,' I said. I'd had a smoke and a drink so I was already pretty relaxed. We pulled up outside a small semi and walked through a back door into a kitchen. Next to the kitchen was a living room with two leather sofas, a TV and a coffee table on which was a litre bottle of vodka, a bottle of Coke and some plastic cups. The place looked like a family home with nice soft furnishings. Imie put the music channel on the TV, sat down on the sofa next to me and poured me a drink.

'Hey, you're really pretty, you know,' he said.

'Oh, thanks.'

'You got beautiful eyes.'

I started to giggle. Imie seemed really nice and this was turning into a fun evening. I drank some more, puffed away on another joint and, after a while, the smoke filling the room made everything seem a little hazy and unclear. I couldn't focus very well but I drank some more booze and the joint was handed to me again, so I had another puff. Imie had his arm around my shoulder and was whispering in my ear. We were laughing together, knocking back vodka and Coke, and then . . . and then . . .

It was the next morning. I woke up in my bed feeling fuzzy and confused. *How did I get home last night? I don't remember coming back here.* I lay there for a while trying to clear the cotton wool from my mind. Everything felt so strange – my head was thick, my mouth was dry and, worryingly, it felt painful *down there*. The light streamed through my curtains, hurting my eyes, so I turned over and checked my phone: 10.21 a.m. I had missed school. Oh well. I racked my brain trying to recall details from the previous night and how I'd got back home. All I remembered was drinking and smoking with Imie at his cousin's house, and then . . . nothing more. It was like the lights went out and I woke up in my bed. I was so worried, I texted Imie: 'What happened last night? How did I get home?'

I didn't want to go to school, so I got up, dressed and took myself to the park where I met Simone and a couple of other friends. It was a grey, drizzly day, so we huddled under the arches of the large stone pavilion and shared fags. There was always someone who had a smoke, and if there wasn't anything to drink one of us would nick a bottle from the corner shop. All day long I kept checking my phone for a reply from Imie but I didn't hear back from him. I felt hurt and a bit confused. I thought we were friends. He seemed so pleased to be with me the day before and I really thought he would let me know what had happened. *Why would he just ignore me like this?* I had an uncomfortable feeling in my gut that we'd messed around together, and that was why I felt sore in my private parts, but I couldn't be sure. I knew he liked me; he'd told me lots of times that I was pretty. If only I could remember . . .

'Where the fuck have you been?' Dad asked when I let myself in that night. He was sat in front of the telly watching the darts.

'Just went to the park, Dad.'

'You taken my weed again?'

'No,' I lied.

'Are you sure you haven't been helping yourself to my weed, because I don't think there's anyone else in this house who smokes apart from you.'

He was right – Tammy didn't do drugs, Mum was no longer in the house and Marie, who did like to smoke, was now living with her partner.

'Dad,' I started. 'I didn't take—'

WHACK!

The smack came completely out of the blue. He'd leapt up out of his chair and walloped me round the head. I was caught off balance and staggered backwards. I felt dizzy and unsteady, and the side of my head throbbed with pain.

'DON'T YOU FUCKING LIE TO ME, CAZ, OR I'LL BEAT THE LIVING CRAP OUT OF YOU,' he exploded.

'Get off, Dad,' I whimpered, then scrambled up the stairs. 'I haven't taken your drugs. Just leave me alone.'

'YOU BETTER FUCKING KEEP YOUR THIEVING HANDS TO YOURSELF,' he shouted up the stairs as I ran into my room and slammed the door behind me, pulling the lock across.

'DON'T TAKE MY FUCKING WEED, YOU ROBBING LITTLE BITCH!'

I stood there, my back against the door, panting and listening for footsteps, hoping he wasn't going to follow me upstairs. I didn't fancy another hiding. Now that Mum was in the care home it felt like he picked on me more. After a couple of minutes I heard the sound of the telly being turned up and the unmistakable click and fizz of a can of lager being opened.

Thank God. He's not going to come up after me tonight. I've got to be more careful in future.

I sighed, relieved, and sunk down onto my bed, then pulled my phone out of my bag and checked my messages again. Still nothing from Imie. Why was he ignoring me? I wanted to talk to someone about it, but who? My sister Tammy wasn't much of a talker – she had moved her girlfriend into our house a few months earlier and they both worked full time, so she was either out working, at the gym or happily tucked up with her girlfriend. My sister Marie had troubles of her own with her partner, Ross, who was violent and aggressive, and Mum was in a care home full time and couldn't speak in any case.

We went to visit her every fortnight and it was really nice to spend time with her. She'd recently moved into a special home for people with Huntington's, so the place was all geared up with the right equipment and the staff there were lovely. They had painted her name on one wall of her room, which was a soft lavender colour, and she had a matching built-in wardrobe, chest of drawers, a TV on one side of the room and a shower and sink on the other. She had a double hospital bed with a frame attached, which allowed the staff to get her in and out of bed easily. I felt happy knowing Mum was being cared for so well. And the staff were good at putting on events to bring the families together.

Not long after Mum moved in, the staff held an Easter party with an egg hunt for the kids of the patients. Marie brought Dara along and all the children raced around the garden, cheered on by their mums and dads, collecting brightly coloured chocolate eggs and yelling with excitement every time they made a discovery. I looked at all the kids, so happy and carefree. It was both lovely and heartbreaking at the same time, as these children didn't have a normal childhood. There was so much they could no longer do with their parent, so many things they couldn't share together – like walking to the shops, enjoying a bedtime story or even a proper cuddle. It was the same for me too, but Mum had been unwell for as long as I could remember, so I'd stopped wanting those things some time ago. Now, seeing her eyes light up as she watched Dara running around made me smile. She could at least share this with her granddaughter. These were little things but I knew they meant a lot to her.

It took just over an hour to get to the care home by car, which would have been fine but Dad was a banned driver and said he couldn't afford to resit his driving test. So every time he drove us there, the journey seemed to go on forever because I was constantly worried he'd get stopped by the police. I just sat in the back, praying for it to be over quickly. Once there, my sisters and I would do Mum's nails, put on her make-up or brush her hair for her. Then I'd hold up a small hand mirror so she could see what we'd done and I knew she was happy. She couldn't smile any more but I could see in her eyes that she was pleased.

Mum could no longer communicate very well but the noises she made and the look in her eyes always told me how she was feeling. She couldn't hold a cigarette any more, so now, when I gave her a fag, I either had to hold it for her or put it in a special ashtray with a tube coming off it that connected to her mouth. Otherwise she would drop it and burn herself. She had scars all over her hands where she had burned herself with her own cigarettes. She also had a special powder in her tea that made it thick enough for her to swallow, and her food had to be blended and fed to her on a baby spoon. In the past she had eaten normal food but her body spasms and involuntary movements had become so strong that the glue wouldn't keep her dentures on her gums, so now she could only eat if the food was blended into a mush.

A couple of months went by and I forgot all about the night with Imie until one afternoon when he messaged me out of the blue: 'Hi Caz – want to meet for a drink?'

I agreed and he picked me up from outside a kebab shop on the Queen's Road later that day. I didn't want him driving too close to my house in case Dad saw and got mad. We shared a joint and I sat with him in his car while he dropped off some weed to another guy. When he got back in the car, I asked him what had happened on the night we'd last seen each other.

He was rolling a joint as he spoke. 'I dropped you home. You were out of it.'

'Yeah? What happened with us though?'

'What? We had sex, that's all,' he said, as he licked the side of the Rizla, then smoothed it down with his fingers. He twisted the thick end of it to stop the gear falling out, popped it into his mouth and flicked open his lighter. He didn't look at me once the whole time.

'Oh, okay,' I said, biting my thumbnail. I didn't know what else to say. I felt odd and a little ashamed for not remembering that we'd had sex. Why couldn't I remember? I wondered why he hadn't replied to my text the following day but I suppose it wasn't a big deal. Like he said, it was just sex.

'So, did we use anything?' I asked. 'I mean, like a condom or something?'

'Nah. Can't stand them things. It's fine, Caz. Don't worry about it.'

'Yeah.' I suppose it was fine. The way he talked about it, it was like it was normal. No big deal. I just wish I had remembered it.

Imie drove us to a pub and we sat outside because it was a sunny day. Then he got up to greet another guy who joined us. He was tall, probably in his mid-forties, with short black hair and a goatee beard. He said his name was also Imie.

'He's my cousin,' Imie laughed. 'I guess you can call us Imie one and Imie two!'

We all laughed and carried on drinking and chatting. It turned out that both the Imies dealt cannabis, so they were usually taking calls or texts on their mobiles. After an hour we all got into Imie 1's car and drove round to a couple of houses to sell weed. We smoked quite a bit too, but I tried not to drink or smoke to excess this time because I didn't want to get so smashed that I didn't know what was happening. Later they dropped me off at the top of my road and I went home feeling happy and high. I put that previous night out of my head completely. It wasn't a big deal, just like Imie said.

One day I was with Tammy, as she had to go to the Jobcentre in town, and Imie 2 texted, asking if I wanted to go for a chill. He picked me up outside the Jobcentre on St James Road, saying he had to make a couple of drop-offs. We drove round Halifax, diving down small roads of identical pale stone houses lined up one after the other. Every ten minutes or so, Imie 2 jumped out, knocked on a door and went inside to do the deal, reappearing a few minutes later. Then he said we were going to a house where he had a 'grow' on. I knew what this was – it was a house where they grew cannabis but no one actually lived there. I knew this because my dad and uncle had done this once in my uncle's house. This was when Mum still lived with us and Dad had made me swear not to tell her anything about it. The funny thing was, Mum was dead against drugs – she always said she'd leave my dad if she ever found out he did them. How on earth she didn't clock that he was stoned half the time I have no idea. She never even smelt it on him and sometimes he reeked of dope.

In my uncle's house they'd taped up all the windows so there was no sunlight going in, but every room had loads of plants with special UV lamps on them to make them grow quicker. I guess after Mum left home Dad wasn't as bothered about her finding out, so he'd grow the plants in the loft of our house. He usually had quite a few growing at any one time – once one lot was finished he'd germinate another batch, so that way he never ran out of dope.

We pulled up in Imie 2's car and he opened the door to the house. I walked in and was immediately hit by the familiar sweet smell of dope. I heard the front door closing behind me and then Imie 2 grabbed me, spun me around and pushed me up against the wall. His hands were all over me, trying to pull my leggings down.

What's going on? I was shocked, too shocked to do anything. 'No!' I started to say, but he was very insistent, pushing me against the staircase with all his weight and tugging at my leggings and knickers at the same time.

'Come on, come on,' he was saying, as he yanked hard at my leggings and pulled my top up with his other hand. The next thing I knew, I was lying on my back against the stairs and my leggings were round my ankles. Then he started touching me *down there*. It felt so wrong. I didn't want it.

'No! No, stop it!' I tried to say, but he pressed his mouth against mine and I couldn't speak. *Urgh*! His mouth tasted sour and smoky. His beard scraped against my chin while the weight of his body crushed me awkwardly against the staircase. I tried to get away but he didn't give me a chance. I couldn't move. I was pinned to the staircase as he put himself inside me.

Jesus! The pain was immense as he pushed himself hard into me. Again and again.

Fuck. Oh God, that hurts.

I just wanted it to be over quickly. It hurt so much. He rammed his body into mine and the impact shoved my back and legs against the steps, hard. I felt the sharp edge of the stairs digging into my back and I whimpered in pain. *Please let it be over soon. Please.* He grunted once, twice and then again. Then his body went floppy and he collapsed on top of me. I hoped that meant it was over.

A few seconds later he pushed himself up off me and, finally, I was free. I scrambled to my feet, pulling up my clothes without a word. I couldn't look at him. I couldn't stay a second longer. I ran out of the house, tears streaking down my face. *Where am I? Where am I?* I felt panicky and scared but I didn't want to risk seeing him again so I dived down a little alleyway, hoping that he wouldn't come after me. Then I ran, left, right and left again, trying to escape between the many lookalike rows of terraced houses. I must have run for about ten minutes, my head down, tears streaming until, finally, I collapsed in a corner, shaking and crying. *Why? Why had he done that to me? I trusted him.*

Eventually, when I had cried my eyes out, I lit a cigarette and drew on it shakily. Then I picked myself up and tried to find my way to a main road so I could figure out where I was.

I got home an hour later. By now it was nearly 8 p.m. but all the lights were off in my house. Either the electricity had gone again or there was nobody home. I let myself in and took myself straight upstairs for a bath. Nobody called out my name so I guessed everyone was out. Thank God! I didn't want to talk to anyone. I felt dirty and ashamed. I ran a hot bath and climbed in, submerging myself completely under the water. Then I picked up the soap and sponge and spent the next ten minutes scrubbing myself top to bottom. I felt really sore inside and out. I was sure my back and legs were covered in bruises but I didn't dare look.

He had raped me. What should I do? Who should I tell?

I thought about the people in my life – Mum wasn't around, Dad wouldn't believe me, or he'd blame me for it. My older sister had too many problems of her own and I didn't feel close enough to Tammy. Besides, what if they didn't believe me? What then?

After my bath I went into Dad's room, found some weed and made a joint, which I smoked out of the bathroom window. Then I lay down on my bed.

Just forget it, I told myself. *Just forget it ever happened. It won't do any good to tell anyone anyway.*

3.

Harry

I WAS ON MY way home from Simone's house when the small green sports car pulled over and the window wound down. It was an Asian man around twenty-five, maybe thirty.

He smiled. 'Hey, how you doing? What have you been up to, beautiful? Out drinking?'

How did he know that? I wondered. I grinned and pulled open my school bag to show him the contents – one half-drunk bottle of vodka.

'Oh right, that's nice,' he laughed. 'You're a vodka girl, are you? I like a bit of a drink myself. You doing anything tonight?'

'Nah, I've just been to see my friend and I'm on my way back home.'

'Well, how do you fancy coming out with me? We could go for a drive or, if you like, I know somewhere we can chill out together.'

He looked nice, this guy, and he seemed really friendly, so I agreed and got into his car. His name was Harry, and we chatted while I swigged on the bottle of vodka.

'There's a place I can take you where we can hang out and have a chill. Do you want to go there?'

'Yeah, why not?'

'Okay, it's not far from here – just a few minutes' drive.'

We swung through the back streets of Halifax, where the green hillsides of the Calder Valley occasionally became visible between the buildings and then disappeared again. After about five minutes we pulled up in front of a small terraced house in the middle of a quiet cobbled road. We got out and Harry knocked. A white man opened the front door.

'Hey, how you doing, man?' They greeted each other with a handshake and a back pat.

'This is Cassie,' Harry said, turning to me, and I gave a little nod.

'And, Cassie, this is the Convert.'

'How you doing?' he asked. The guy was tall, skinny and had a long beard. I guessed they called him the Convert because he was wearing Asian clothes and had obviously converted to Islam at some point. He welcomed us into the house. We walked through to the living room, which had a small lounge with an old gas fire. The decor looked a little old and careworn but the Convert seemed like a very friendly guy. He and Harry sat down, took out some weed and started rolling joints.

We talked a little and I found out that the Convert used to be married and he had two little girls but they now lived with their mum. I reckoned he was older than Harry, probably in his mid-forties. Harry told me he was twenty-seven. I finished off the vodka and Harry asked me if I liked to have a smoke.

'Yeah, sure,' I said, so we all smoked some weed. The Convert turned the TV onto the music channel and we all just smoked and chilled out. It was a really nice night. Later, I went upstairs to use the toilet. As I came out, I met Harry on the stairs.

'Cassie, it's been really nice tonight, you know, getting to know you and everything,' he said. 'Do you fancy meeting up again, just you and me?'

'Yeah, why not?'

'That's great. I'll text you another time.'

'Sure. But I think I better be getting home now. Can you take me back? I've got school tomorrow.'

'Yeah, no problem.'

So I gathered up my things and Harry took me home in his car. I had enjoyed myself – they both seemed like nice guys. Harry told me that he and his brother Ti dealt a little cannabis but they gave it to the Convert for free, and that's why he let them use his house.

He dropped me on the corner of Queen's Road and I walked the rest of the way home. Then, as quietly as possible, I snuck into the house, hoping not to wake Dad. He'd been in a terrible mood recently, giving me a hiding for anything and everything. A week earlier I'd had a pen fight on the bus to school with my friends and, unfortunately, it turned out to be permanent marker, so a couple of the girls couldn't get the pen marks out of their white school shirts. Luckily I didn't get hit too badly but the following Monday evening there was a knock on the door and it was my friend Kayley's mum. Kayley was standing next to her, an apologetic smile on her face. Her mum, on the other hand, looked really angry, and in a tight-lipped way she asked to speak to my dad.

'Dad! Someone at the door for you!' I yelled into the living room. It took a couple of minutes for Dad to sort himself out and, when he got to the front door, he didn't look happy.

'Yeah, what's the problem?' he asked gruffly, already pissed off for being dragged away from the horse racing.

'Mr Pike, the problem is that your daughter and some of her friends thought it would be funny to put pen marks all over my Kayley's clothes,' Kayley's mum started. 'Permanent marker pen! So now her school uniform is completely ruined. See!'

She then shoved the pen-covered shirt in our direction. I took it from her and gently turned it over, a little confused. There were several large grey stains on the front. But we hadn't drawn the pen all over her in particular. She made it sound as if we were all picking on Kayley, but that wasn't true – it was just one big pen fight and Kayley had joined in. She just happened to get more pen on her shirt than the rest of us.

Dad took the shirt off me and turned it over, furrowing his brow as Kayley's mum continued speaking: 'I've had to go out and buy a new shirt for Kayley, as well as a new skirt, which is money I really don't have to spare. The whole lot came to twenty-two pounds. Now tell me, who's going to pay me back that money?'

Dad scowled then handed the shirt back to Kayley's mum and scratched his beard. Finally he turned to me. 'Well, Cassie? What have you got to say for yourself? That's a fucking ruined uniform, that is.'

'Dad, it wasn't just me. There was a whole bunch of us—' I started, but I didn't get any further. He walloped me on the back of the head.

'I said, WHAT HAVE YOU GOT TO SAY FOR YOURSELF?' he shouted. 'DO YOU PAY FOR THIS GIRL'S SCHOOL UNIFORM? YOU FUCKING RUINED IT! WHAT DO YOU SAY?' And then he smashed me on the head again.

'I'm sorry!' I yelped. 'I'm really sorry. Ow, Dad! Get off me!' But it was too late – he was really wound up and was going for it, smacking me about the head over and over again. I cowered next to him in the doorway as the blows came thick and fast.

'You fucking cheeky bitch. Look what you did, for fuck's sake! As if I haven't got enough shit to deal with without you playing up!'

Between the blows I glimpsed Kayley and her mum still standing at the front door, only now the mum didn't look quite so angry. In fact, she looked really alarmed.

'Look, Mr Pike, you really don't have to –' she started to say, as he walloped me again. 'I mean, well, her apology is fine. That's all. I just wanted to hear . . .'

I didn't hear anything more because at that point I ran inside. Dad chased after me while she was left standing at the door. I managed to get up the stairs and into my room before he could do anything more, but still he shouted after me and, not long afterwards, I heard the front door slam. Outside I could hear the distinct clicking of heels on pavement as Kayley and her mother walked away, Kayley saying, 'I told you he'd do that!'

'I know. I wish we hadn't come now.'

A couple of days later, Harry texted me again, asking me if I wanted to meet up. He picked me up from outside the Asia Superstore on Queen's Road and we went to the Convert's house again. There was more booze, more dope and, after a while, I went upstairs to go to the toilet. When I came out Harry led me into the bedroom next to the bathroom and started to kiss me.

'I like you, Cassie,' he said, as he pushed me back onto the bed. 'You like me too, don't you?'

I couldn't reply because he was kissing my mouth and pulling off my clothes at the same time. He was forceful, shoving my jeans down while lying on top of me so I couldn't move. It all happened so quickly I hardly had time to think and, before I knew it, he was having sex with me. I didn't say no. I guess I went with it because Harry seemed nice and he said he liked me.

We met up a few more times, always at the Convert's house, for a smoke and sex. He talked to me about his brother Ti and said I should meet him one day. One evening, after I'd gone upstairs to use the toilet, I met two small girls on the landing. They looked to be around five and six years old and they both stared at me with large, curious eyes.

'Hello,' I said in a friendly voice, but they didn't respond. One of them clutched a small, scruffy teddy and the other hid her face behind long curtains of hair. They scurried across the landing and into their room. I was puzzled, as I thought we were the only people in the house.

'I've just met two little girls up there,' I told the Convert when I came back down.

'Oh yeah, they're my kids,' he said matter-of-factly. 'Are they still awake? I told them to go to sleep ages ago.'

'They're really sweet,' I said.

'Yeah, but their mum's a bitch!' he replied, with real venom.

I had nothing else to say to that, so I grabbed the bottle of vodka and took a swig. I had sex with Harry that night, and a couple of times after that too.

'Hi, Ti is picking u up tonight. I'll c u later at the Convert's house.'

I read the text as I walked along the Queen's Road. Me and Harry had been friends for a few months now. I liked him and he was always generous about buying me booze and giving me dope. I'd never met his brother before, so I didn't know who to look for when I stood outside the Asia Superstore. Luckily Ti seemed to recognise me.

'You Cassie?' he called out from his sleek black Audi.

'Yes.'

'Alright, get in. Let's go and buy some booze first.'

I climbed into the passenger seat and saw that Ti was short and stocky and, like many other Asian guys, had a small goatee. He was wearing jeans and a blue T-shirt and seemed a bit younger than Harry. Behind him was another Asian guy who Ti introduced as his friend Ash.

'Yeah, Harry couldn't come and get you because he picked up a girl last night,' he said, grinning at me. 'Some girl called Sam. Do you know her?'

'No.'

'Nor do I. She's probably really ugly. My brother only picks up ugly girls.'

I looked at him and he started to laugh. I didn't know if he was joking or not so I just ignored his last comment. We pulled up at a small corner shop. At that moment Harry also pulled up in his car and I saw that he had a girl in the back. This was obviously Sam. Harry went into the shop and came out with a few bottles of vodka. Then we drove in convoy to the Convert's house and Harry let us in.

We all sat in the living room, having a drink and a smoke. And this time someone brought out some fet. I knew what fet was because I'd had it a few times in the park – it was amphetamine. We wrapped it in a Rizla and then swallowed it. The fet went round, and after a while I found myself getting really talkative and giggly. Someone was playing music from their phone and it felt like a party. I found myself speaking to Sam. She lived in a street not far from my house. She was a little older than me at fifteen but seemed really nice and friendly.

The party was in full swing when Harry, who was sitting next to me, suddenly stood up and got his penis out. Then he started playing with himself. I was a bit shocked at first. I looked at Sam, who rolled her eyes at me as if to say, *It's a bit odd, but there you go!* Yes, it *was* odd, but nobody else batted an eyelid. They all acted like it was completely normal – smoking, drinking and chatting as before, in Urdu, I think. Harry swung himself in my direction and I swerved to avoid him, then I laughed it off. *Oh well, if nobody else thinks it's a big deal . . . I suppose I should just go with it.* We were all pretty high by that point, so I guessed he was just a little out of it. After a minute or so he put his penis back in his trousers and we all just went on as before.

The Convert wasn't at home that day, which was a bit strange because he had been there every other time I'd come. I heard the heavy rain clattering at the window and felt relieved that I'd decided not to stay in the park. Thank God I had a warm dry house to sit in!

'I'm bursting for the toilet,' Sam announced after a while, laughing.

'Yeah, me too,' I said. So we both got up and staggered upstairs to the bathroom together.

'Fuck! I nearly fell down the stairs!' Sam giggled as she lost her footing a couple of times. I was also struggling to put one foot in front of the other. God, I'm really wasted, I thought to myself, as I tried hard to focus on climbing the stairs. At least we were together. After what felt like ages, Sam and I got to the bathroom and managed to both go for a wee. We were giggling a lot but we didn't even know why. Probably because we were both really off our faces.

After we'd finished, I opened the bathroom door and was surprised to see both Harry and Ti standing there waiting for us, smiling. I didn't have time to say anything as Harry took Sam by the shoulders and guided her to one bedroom while Ti took me to the other.

'Come on, Caz,' Ti said gently, as he held me by the arms and walked me into the bedroom. I didn't know what was happening, so I just let myself be led. And then he pushed me backwards onto the bed and closed the door behind him.

'What?' I started to say, but Ti interrupted me.

'Don't worry about it, Caz. It's fine with Sam. She's cool with it.'

Oh right, I thought dreamily to myself, as he took down his trousers and climbed on top of me. *I guess if Sam's cool with it then I should be too. So I guess he's going to have sex with me . . .*

I must have lost consciousness because the next thing I knew Ti was gone and Ash had come into the room. I looked at him blearily. *What's he doing here?* He took down his trousers and the next thing I knew he was also on top of me. *Fuck, I feel really wasted.* I blacked out again and every time I woke up it felt like someone else was in the room. It was Harry, then Ti, then Ash. They all seemed to merge into one and I couldn't keep track of what was going on. Just go with it, Cassie, I told myself. Everything felt so blurry and strange. I lay back on the bed and closed my eyes as the room spun around me and the men came and went.

I finally woke up with full awareness, realising I had come round properly. There was no one else there, no music coming from downstairs. It was just me in the room. I shivered with cold. *What time is it?* The stillness in the air made me think it was quite late but I had no idea. I slowly rolled onto my side and pulled myself up to a sitting position. My clothes were scattered around the room, so I gathered them up and put them back on. Everything seemed to be happening in slow motion and I could feel myself swaying as I sat on the bed. I put my hand to my head and felt my hair was all messed up. Then I stood up, feeling achy and painful down my legs and groin. I winced in pain as I walked carefully out of the room, across the corridor and towards the other bedroom. Tentatively I pushed open the door. Sam was in there, asleep, covered by a single sheet.

'Sam?' I called out softly. 'Sam? Are you okay?' I guessed they had been coming in to have sex with her too.

'Oh,' she groaned. I sat down on the bed next to her.

'Are you alright, Sam?' I whispered, putting a hand on her shoulder.

'Yeah, yeah. I'll be fine.'

'Did they all come in here?'

'Yeah, they did.'

'All of them?'

'I ... uh ... I think so.'

'Come on, Sam, let's go.'

I helped to find her clothes and she got dressed. Then the two of us got our stuff together and we left. I had been to the Convert's house enough times now to know how to get home, so I just walked back in the dark, trying my best to shield myself from the rain. I felt horrible about what had happened. It wasn't nice, but then I guessed that if Sam was okay about it then maybe I should be too. We didn't speak much on the way back – I felt a little ashamed of what had happened and shocked too. How many times had they had sex with me? I didn't even know.

Well, I suppose I could have said no but I didn't, so it was my fault really. I'd let them do it. Sam didn't seem to have a problem with it so I guess that what happened was normal. Still, I didn't feel good. I just wanted to go home to my own bed and forget it ever happened.

When I finally managed to crawl into bed it was just gone four in the morning. I curled up into a tight ball and thought about my mum. She hadn't been home in ages now. I don't think she could any more – she needed too much care and Dad couldn't cope. I recalled one weekend when she'd been home and I'd come downstairs in the middle of the night to get a glass of water to find her sprawled on the floor of the living room. How had she got down there? I started to wonder, but then I saw my dad's hand reach down, grab hold of her hair and pull her head back. Her mouth hung open, there was a flash of silver, and I saw that he had a knife to her throat. I gasped, and that's when he saw me.

'Get back to bed!' he hissed.

I hesitated in the doorway for a second, paralysed, not knowing what to do. My mum was just lying there, unable to scream, incapable of getting away. Tammy appeared next to me. She'd been woken by the noise and had come downstairs to find out what was happening. Now the pair of us stood side by side in the doorway, petrified, not knowing what to do. We couldn't just leave her.

'I SAID GET BACK UPSTAIRS, THE PAIR OF YOU, OR SO HELP ME, I'LL FUCKING RUIN YOU!' Dad thundered.

We both scampered back up the stairs, praying that Dad wouldn't hurt her with the knife. I lay awake for hours that night, hoping Dad had calmed down enough to let Mum alone. Her grunts and noises reassured me that at least she was still alive, and thankfully she seemed okay the next day. But it had been awful to see her like that – helpless and defenceless. Yes, I suppose it was for the best she was in the home and away from our place. Away from Dad and his violent temper.

4.

Loss

ONE DAY IN LATE August 2008, not long after my thirteenth birthday, Dad announced that he was taking me and Tammy ice skating. I was a little amazed, frankly, because he never did anything with us, let alone take us to a fun activity. I'd been skating once before, but not with him, so I knew how to do it. When I was younger I'd had a care worker called Sandra, who took me out a few times to take part in fun activities. I'd wobbled, skidded and screamed on the ice as she held my hand and I'd loved every minute. Ice skating was fun! In fact, Sandra had taken me out for other exciting activities like canoeing and rock climbing with other children from the area, all of which I had loved. But I'd never done anything like that with Dad. Could he even skate? I had no idea.

'Can Claire come with us?' I asked, excitedly.

'What?' Dad looked a bit nonplussed.

'Claire!' I pointed to my friend who had come over for the

afternoon. She was standing right next to me and I knew it would be even more fun if she came too.

'No,' Dad said.

'Why not? There's a spare seat in the car.'

He hesitated for a second and then sighed. 'Oh, alright. Claire can come too, I suppose. Just get in the car.'

So we all jumped in. Claire rode up front next to Dad while me and Tammy sat next to each other in the back. This was great! I couldn't remember the last time we'd been for a family outing with Dad. It was just a shame Marie and Dara weren't with us. I wondered if I could remember how to skate and whether I would fall over. You had to keep your fingers tucked in if you fell over, I knew that. Now I babbled excitedly to Claire.

'You have to make your hands into fists if you fall on your bum,' I said. 'Or someone else could come along and skate over your fingers and chop them off! So if you fall over, just keep your fingers in, right!'

'Like this?' She showed me a balled fist.

'Yes, exactly. Like that.'

Dad remained silent as he drove us to the skating rink in Bradford, parked in the car park and then switched the engine off. I opened the door to get out.

'Get back in the car, Caz,' Dad ordered.

'Why?'

'I've got some news, that's why.'

He suddenly went very quiet and looked down at his hands. *Was he crying? What's going on?* Tammy and I looked at each other, concerned.

He gave a huge, shaky sigh and then, in a quiet voice, he said, 'I'm really sorry, girls, but your mum's died.'

Died? What did he mean? I was confused. I couldn't take in what was going on.

'But, Dad, why have you brought us ice skating?' I asked.

'We're not going ice skating, Cassie. I just wanted to bring you somewhere quiet to break the news.'

A huge silence filled the car as we all sat trying to absorb the horrible news.

'When did she die, this morning?' I asked in a small voice.

He sighed again. 'No, a couple of days ago.'

A couple of days ago? This was even stranger. I just couldn't understand what was going on.

'Dad, why didn't you tell us a couple of days ago?'

'I don't know. I was trying to get my head around it.'

I was completely shattered. My poor mum was dead, but worse, I didn't even know about it because Dad decided he needed time to get his head together. Now he'd decided to tell us after announcing he was taking us ice skating. I had got excited about going ice skating. I'd even insisted on bringing my poor friend along. Now Tammy collapsed into floods of tears, weeping into her hands while Claire sat in an awkward silence in the front passenger seat and Dad got out the car to light a fag.

I watched him pulling up his collar and then he cupped his hand around his lighter and blew a puff of smoke into the air. Mum was gone. I thought about the last time I'd seen her – it had been ages ago. I was meant to see her on her forty-seventh birthday a couple of weeks earlier but that whole trip had ended in disaster. The plan was for all of us to go and see her – not just the immediate family but also my uncle, aunt and some cousins. For some reason that I didn't understand Dad decided to go in my uncle's car with my sisters while my uncle drove Dad's car. So I was with my uncle and four other members of the family, and all the presents were in the back for the one-hour drive to the care home. We were on the motorway when the police pulled us over.

'Oh shit!' My uncle swore when he saw the blue flashing lights in his rear-view mirror.

'What's wrong? Why are they pulling us over?' I asked, but he didn't answer me.

Actually, it didn't take long to find out what the problem was. The two policemen told us straight away that the car didn't have a MOT, tax or insurance. I sighed. So that's why Dad didn't want to drive his car. If he had been driving it, he would have been arrested because not only was his car on the road illegally, he didn't have a licence. I was fuming as I watched the police take charge of the vehicle. Why was Dad incapable of doing anything properly? The irony was that he and my sisters got to see my mum that day but we didn't because his car was seized and we all had to go home in a taxi. Mum didn't even get any presents. Now, three weeks later, she was dead. I felt the tears welling up behind my eyes. It wasn't fair. She'd had such a hard life and she hadn't even had any presents on her birthday.

'Come on.' Dad was now back in the car. He started the engine. 'Let's go home.'

Once we were back, I went upstairs to my bedroom and Claire came in after me.

'I'm really sorry about your mum, Caz,' she said, sitting down next to me on the bed. 'That was all wrong. I shouldn't have been there when he told you.'

'It's not your fault. You weren't to know. I just wish he'd told us when it actually happened. I don't understand why he had to wait. I feel bad that she's been dead all this time and I didn't know.'

'I had a feeling something had happened,' Claire said. 'You remember I was here a couple of days ago?'

I nodded.

'Well, I think it was like three or four in the afternoon and I was in the kitchen. The phone went and your dad took it and then he closed the kitchen door so I couldn't hear what he was saying. Then, well, I could have sworn I heard him crying. And afterwards he walked out the house. Do you remember? Your cousin's boyfriend was here and your uncle.'

It was coming back to me now. That was a strange afternoon, I remember.

'They were taking down the net curtains in the living room and putting them in the washing machine,' I recalled. 'They started doing loads of cleaning all of a sudden. Taking the cushion covers off and washing them too.'

'Yeah.' Claire nodded. 'That's right.'

'And then my uncle gave me twenty quid and said, 'Here you go – buy yourself something nice.' Everyone was being really kind to me that day.' I started to put two and two together.

'I think that was the day it happened,' Claire said.

'And I took his twenty quid, went out and bought some

booze and got drunk in the park,' I concluded. I felt so sad now, thinking about that day and how I'd just got drunk without knowing what was really going on. Dad had also disappeared that day, probably getting drunk himself somewhere. I knew he loved her, in his own way. After all, they'd been together since they were thirteen years old and she hadn't always been ill. For some reason they had never married but they had stayed together all that time and I guess that counted for something. But he just couldn't cope towards the end and he took his frustration out on her.

We held a big funeral for her in a church just outside Halifax. During the service me and my sisters stood around the coffin, on top of which was a picture of her and a flower arrangement that spelled out 'Mum'. We all cried a lot. Even though we knew Mum didn't have much of a life towards the end, she was still our mother and we loved her. She had loved us too and had done her best even though the illness had taken everything from her. Afterwards we went to the pub for the wake and everyone got drunk. Even though I was still only thirteen, Tammy and Marie bought me a vodka and Coke each while my dad bought me a lager.

I told Tammy how bad I felt about missing Mum's birthday a few weeks earlier, and she reminded me about her birthday party the year before.

'It was great, do you remember?'

'Yeah, I do.' I grinned.

It was 2007 and Mum had only been in the new care home for a short time but, still, they threw a massive surprise birthday party for her, inviting all the patients and their families. We all went along – me, Dad, my sisters, as well as my aunt and two cousins. They laid on a big buffet in the living room with music, balloons and birthday decorations and then, about halfway through, they announced that there was a special visitor for my mum and all the adults had to go through to another room. I was still just twelve years old but for some reason they let me join my mum as they wheeled her chair through. I was curious about this special guest. Who on earth could it be?

Mum was next to me in her massive comfy wheelchair when the policeman came in and I saw her eyes widen in surprise. He was quite tall with short brown hair and he was carrying a stereo. Suddenly, some of the adults in the room started to giggle. A policeman? Why was a policeman a special guest at mum's party?

''Ello 'ello 'ello. I'm PC Tease and I hear there's been some trouble around here,' he said a loud voice, placing his stereo down. 'One Elizabeth Pike has been up to no good. So I'm here to take down her particulars and put her in cuffs!' At that point the policeman switched on the music, ripped open the front of his shirt to reveal a six-pack and pulled out a pair of fluffy black handcuffs. A few of the women screamed and I caught on that he wasn't a real copper, he was a stripper. My mum's eyes danced with delight – she looked so happy.

PC Tease strutted around the room and swung his hips really close to Mum's head. It was the closest I'd seen to a smile in months. She was having the time of her life. The stripper had a really good body, which was tanned and oiled, and he danced around the room, inviting the women to stroke his chest.

Gradually he took off all his clothes until he was down to just a pair of black pants. I was laughing really hard and the other women in the room were screaming and wolf-whistling. Then PC Tease danced really close to my mum, swinging his pants towards her face and everyone screamed harder. Mum was really happy and excited. It was a great afternoon and we took loads of pictures of her with the stripper. Later we all sat around Mum in her room and opened her presents for her. Now Tammy and I both smiled at the memory.

'We had some good times, didn't we?' I said.

'Yeah.'

'I miss her,' I said sadly.

'Me too,' said Tammy. 'I've missed her for a long time.'

After the funeral I didn't see Dad all that much. He was out a lot and, when he was at home, he was usually off his face. He seemed to be drinking more, smoking more weed and doing more fet too. One morning, a couple of months after the funeral, I was cleaning out the fitted wardrobes in Mum's bedroom when I came across a heavy book on a shelf that I'd not seen before. 'Baby book' it said on the front. Perhaps it's mine, I wondered. I opened it and inside there was a birth certificate, an umbilical cord and a pair of baby handprints and footprints. But the name on the birth certificate wasn't mine – it was for a Clementine Pike. I was confused. *Who is Clementine Pike?* I took the book downstairs and showed it to Tammy.

'I found this upstairs in Mum's wardrobe,' I said. 'Who is it?'

'Oh, right,' Tammy said, and took the book from me. She leafed through it, nodding sadly.

'Who is it?' I asked again.

She stayed silent for a moment, tracing the outline of the tiny footprints with her finger.

'It's our sister,' she said quietly. 'She died when she was just a baby. Mum got pregnant when you were about five or six. I must have been about fourteen. But she was already quite ill and was walking with the sticks. Towards the end of the pregnancy she was out in town when she fell down two flights of concrete steps. The ambulance took her to hospital and Mum went into labour straight away. She had the baby, a little girl, and she was alive when she was born but she didn't make it. She died shortly after the birth.'

I was shocked. This was my sister? I couldn't believe I didn't know about this younger sister of mine – Clementine. I racked my brain to try and come up with a memory of seeing Mum with a large, pregnant belly but I couldn't for the life of me summon up the image.

'Why didn't I know?' I asked. 'Why didn't anyone tell me I had another sister?'

Tammy shrugged. 'Dunno. They didn't want to upset you, I guess. Nobody talked about her. It was just a very sad thing. Mum used to go the church where they buried her – she used to take flowers there. And that's where we had the funeral for Mum, the same place they buried Clementine. Dad tells me they're going to scatter Mum's ashes over her grave.'

I was stunned at this news. There was so much I didn't know. Why hadn't anyone told me I had a sister? Why had I found out accidentally, just from cleaning the cupboards? I was at the very place she was buried and nobody had even bothered to point out her grave to me. I was flooded with emotion: sadness, anger, confusion, and also guilt that I'd never even known about her until this moment. It struck me that I could have gone years without knowing. I might never have found out.

'She must have been very sad about the baby,' I murmured.

'Yeah, she was. When she got too ill to go to the graveside herself, she asked me to go for her. She never forgot her little Clemmie,' Tammy said. 'I think she felt guilty, or something, like it was her fault. But it really wasn't. There was nothing she could have done.'

That night I lay in bed and thought about my mum and all the sadness she had endured in her life – first losing her own mother and sisters and then having a disease which took away her movements and ability to speak, and even took her baby girl. *Clemmie.* Perhaps it was for the best that Mum wasn't around to suffer any more. She could understand everything you said, but by the end she could no longer communicate with us at all. She just had to sit there, locked into a world of silence. It must have been so hard for her.

I wondered what it would have been like to have a younger sister. I suppose I would have had to look after her myself since Mum wasn't able to do it. But I liked looking after young children, so I wouldn't have minded. Maybe a little sister would have been fun. I certainly would have appreciated another child in the house. Growing up I felt lonely so much of the time. It always felt like everyone else was so much older than me.

I soon found out that Dad had a new girlfriend and that was why he was away so much. I barely saw him these days, and Marie and Tammy had their own lives. So I went to the park, met up with Simone and my friends, listened to music and got high. The new school year began but I didn't tell any of the teachers about mum dying – why should I? Dad had hammered it into me that I wasn't to talk to people in authority, so I tended to keep myself to myself. In November Dad moved out of the house altogether, saying he was going to live with his girlfriend permanently, so now it was up to Tammy and her girlfriend to pay the bills and look after his cannabis plants. I didn't have any say in the matter and, to be honest, I was pretty pleased he was leaving.

Even though I was still only thirteen, life was easier when he wasn't around. I could stay out for as long as I liked and there was nobody to tell me off or beat me up if I came home late. If it meant there was less money around to buy food or feed the electricity meter, well, that was just the price of freedom. Anyway, I was pretty good at taking care of myself. I'd been doing it all my life, so I didn't have any problem with Dad leaving home. I was out most nights, meeting up with friends or cruising with guys in their cars. They usually offered me something to drink or a smoke, and that meant I could always find a way to get high. Life was easier when I was high. I could forget about Mum, forget about home and just relax.

5.

My Normal

'DO I THINK THAT'S *what*?' I struggled to make sense of what the youth worker Adam was saying to me.

'I said, do you think that's *normal*?' he repeated. 'Bringing drugs into school. Is that normal?'

Normal. The word swirled around in my head. *Normal. Normal. What's normal?* What was this all about, anyway? Adam had seen me a couple of times before, but he'd been called in specially by the school in early April 2009 because I'd been caught giving cannabis to some of the other kids. It wasn't much – just a few buds from my dad's plants – but the way the school went on about it you'd think I'd murdered someone. They even called the police on me, but since I was only thirteen there wasn't much they could do. Besides, I told them the truth – the dope was from my dad's plants, so if they had a problem with that they better speak to him. Ha! Good luck with that, I thought. I never saw him these days, so I doubted the police had much chance of catching up with him. The only time he bothered to come back to the house was to check on his beloved plants – and, of course, if me or Tammy forgot to turn the lights on or off then he'd give us a good hiding for it. I felt I had every right to take some of his dope – after all, I was helping him grow the stuff. So while the police went off to look for my dad, the school called in Adam to have a 'little chat' with me. Now his brow furrowed in concern, as he asked how things were at home.

'Yeah, fine,' I replied.

'How's your mum?'

'Mum's dead.'

'Oh.' He looked shocked and a little embarrassed as he rifled through his notes. 'She's dead? I . . . I didn't know. I'm so sorry. What about your dad?'

I shrugged.

'Your dad's still alive, isn't he?'

'Probably,' I sighed. 'I don't see him much these days. He moved out of the house at the end of last year, so I'm now living with Tammy, my sister, and her girlfriend Thea.'

'How old is Tammy?'

'She's twenty-one.'

At least I still had Tammy. She was the one constant in my life these days. I still saw Marie and Dara every week or so, but her partner Ross wasn't very nice to her and it was hard to be around them when he was in a bad mood. If I saw Dad at all, he was usually wasted – he took a lot of drugs these days: M-CAT, fet, coke, cannabis . . . anything he could get his hands on. I'd met his new girlfriend once or twice – she seemed okay and Dad really liked her, but she was a recovering alcoholic and had two sons of her own. I went round to her house a couple of times to ask him for money. I knew he would find it difficult to refuse me if I asked him in front of her. He didn't want to look mean, and it wasn't like he ever gave me much anyway – the odd twenty quid here or there. I could spend that in one night on booze.

Now Adam fell silent as he flicked through the notes in his file, biting his nails, looking confused. My head ached. *Urgh, how much longer do I have to sit here? It's such a waste of time.* I'd been out the night before and I now had a banging headache. I was dying for a fag. My hand reached inside my school bag and I felt around for the pack of ten Regals I'd bought last night on my way home. I clasped the small pack in my hand. *Come on . . . come on.* I hated being in situations like this, and I hated being questioned.

'So, who cooks for you? Who cleans your clothes?' he asked.

I shrugged again. I'd been doing my own cooking and cleaning since I was eight years old. 'I do it myself,' I told him. 'My dad never did it anyway, even before he moved out.'

'Do you miss him?'

'No!' I scoffed. 'He was horrible to me when he lived at home. He always hit me and my sister so I was pleased he moved out. Look, I don't want to say anything else about my dad, okay? Because if I start talking I won't stop and then he would end up in prison!' I laughed. It was sort of a joke and not a joke at the same time. Adam didn't smile; instead he made a note in his file.

'Is that it?' I stood up impatiently and hauled my book bag over my shoulder. I'd had enough of this rubbish. I just wanted to leave.

'Not quite, Cassie. Sit down.'

I flopped back down on the chair. He was pissing me off, this Adam guy. I just didn't understand what all the fuss was about. *Everybody smokes weed, don't they? Everybody I know, anyway.* The corner shops near us sported brightly coloured bongs in their windows, just underneath the Paw Patrol toys and next to the children's tea sets. If you walked along the Queen's Road at any time of day, the only thing you could smell were takeaway kebabs and dope. Yes, that was normal. Smoking dope was normal where I lived. I had smoked it before I even tried a cigarette. It just wasn't a big deal.

'Cassie, I can see your school attendance record isn't all that great. Tell me, what do you do at night?' Adam had started on a new line of questioning. I stared at him, hard.

'What do you mean?'

'I mean, do you stay at home with your sister watching *Corrie*? Do you see your friends? Do you do any activities like sports, clubs or go to any special groups at all? Are you a member of a church or a youth group? How do you fill your hours out of school?'

'My sister works a lot. She's got a packing job at the moment so she's on shift work most nights. I guess I like to meet my friends in the park or go cruising with guys.'

'Cruising? What do you mean, "cruising"?'

'Oh, you know, just hanging out with guys in their cars. Nothing special. Just chilling.'

Adam nodded, his pen poised over his notebook. 'So, these guys that you chill with – they have cars?'

I nodded.

'And you go driving around with them?'

'Yup.'

'And that's all you do?'

I shrugged. I wasn't going to tell him anything more. After all, I didn't want to get anyone into trouble.

'And does your sister know about this?' Adam asked.

'Sure. She's fine with it.' And it was true – Tammy often asked me where I was going. I'd tell her I was going out to chill with some guy and she would say, 'Okay, but be careful. You should be careful about getting into cars with guys.' I didn't know what she meant about that. Most of the guys I knew were really nice and they always shared their booze and drugs with me. I stood up. I'd had enough of this.

'Are we done here?'

'Yeah, sure, Cassie, we're done. Look after yourself, okay?'

'I always do!' I smiled back and left.

School was over for the day, so I walked through the gates and lit up a fag. Thank God that was over! I didn't like being questioned – it made me feel like I was a criminal, especially the way he'd said the word 'normal'. Was it normal to smoke weed and go out at night? It was for me. These days I usually met Simone, Claire or one of my other friends in the park, and we always ended up getting high or drunk. I never had to worry about being careful because nobody was ever threatening or violent towards me. Not like my dad or Ross! The guys I hooked up with were all really nice. They'd pull up in a car while I was walking home or, if they saw me in the park, sitting on top of one of the benches with my mates, they'd come over and start chatting to me. They'd ask if I wanted to go for a drink or a smoke and a chill. They were kind and said nice things to me, complimented me on my figure, or my eyes, and often they told me I was beautiful. They offered to buy me drinks or shared their drugs with me. Sometimes I'd end up in a house or even a hotel and then, maybe, towards the end of the evening, I'd find myself having sex with one of the guys. That was always later on, when I was wrecked, and by then I was usually so out of it I'd black out. Half the time I couldn't remember the sex itself but it wasn't a big deal. It was normal.

Not long after that little chat with Adam, I got in trouble with the police again. It was a balmy night in August 2009 and I was out having fun. I'd been sunbathing in the park most of the afternoon with Simone and her cousin Angela, from Huddersfield, while we listened to music and smoked a few joints. When we got too hot we hid under the shade of the horse chestnut tree, dipped our toes in the large fountain in the middle of the park or disappeared into the bushy hillocks where nobody could see us. There we'd spark up our joints and drink vodka. There were some of the usual guys hanging around on the benches surrounding the fountains, and occasionally they'd come up and start chatting to one of us. One guy, called Kay, was Asian, mid-twenties, not bad looking, and I'd spoken to him a few times before.

'Hey, girls!' He approached us at around 9 p.m., just as it was getting dark, and the three of us, shivering in our small shorts and T-shirts, were thinking about heading home. 'What are you up to tonight? Do you fancy coming to my house? Have a little drink and a party with a few guys I know?'

I looked at Simone, who nodded, and Angela also seemed up for it.

'Yes, sure,' I said. 'Why not?'

'Great. It's not far from here. We can walk.'

So we all got up and followed Kay as he led us out of the park and towards his house. On the way he checked his phone and sent some texts. As we approached the corner shop, he asked if any of us had booze. We all shook our heads.

'Alright, let's get something to drink, then. Don't worry about it, I'll pay.'

So we picked up a litre bottle of vodka and a small bottle of whisky, along with a couple of bottles of pop. Kay led us down some backstreets and finally we got to his house – a small, end of terrace with a broken gate. Me, Simone and Angela were all giggling as we fell through the front door and walked into the living room where there were three guys already sitting in the lounge. They all stood up and looked at Kay as we stumbled in.

'Alright, fellas?' Kay grinned at them and they nodded. I'd never seen any of these guys in my life before and neither had Simone. We sat down in the middle of the room and Kay poured the booze into little plastic cups. Me, Simone and Angela all started drinking and asked them to turn the music on. The other guys were really quiet – they were Asian, probably in their mid-forties, and they all just sat on the sofa, hands folded, not speaking much. I got the impression that they couldn't understand what we were saying.

'Hey, Kay, where's your bathroom?' I asked, as I stood up

woozily. I'd been out in the sun most of the day, drinking, so now I was really quite drunk. Kay pointed upwards.

'Just go up the stairs and turn left. It's at the end of the corridor.'

I staggered out of the room and blinked against stark corridor lighting. A single bare bulb hung from overhead. I went up the stairs and turned left, just as Kay instructed, though it wasn't easy, as I was so drunk. There were several doors on the way to the toilet and they were all padlocked. Weird, I thought to myself. Then, just as I was getting to the loo, one of the padlocked doors opened and an old Asian man peeked out from behind it.

'Alright?' I asked him. He just shook his head and put his hands up. I guessed that meant he didn't understand what I was saying. *Fucking hell. What an odd night.*

Back downstairs I drank some more vodka while Kay tried to sweet-talk Simone into going upstairs with him.

'Come on, darling. Let's go. Just you and me,' he whispered to her over and over, his arm around her shoulder.

'In a minute,' she giggled. 'Let me finish my drink first.'

'You don't need another drink.'

'I do.'

'You're gorgeous, you know . . .'

I didn't talk to any of the guys on the sofa. I got the feeling they didn't really speak English, so I just drank and chatted to Angela. Eventually Kay managed to get Simone to her feet. He led her upstairs as she swayed and stumbled around. The music was blaring out, me and Angela were completely blasted, and then I saw a flashing blue light streaming in through the window. That's strange, I thought blearily to myself. Why is there a blue light at the window? Then . . .

BANG, BANG, BANG! Three loud thuds on the door, followed by: 'POLICE, OPEN UP!'

Angela and I looked at each other in surprise. The police. Why were they here? The three guys on the sofa looked comically alarmed, and I almost laughed at their panic-stricken faces as they stood up and sat down again, uncertain what to do. I shrugged. I hadn't done anything wrong. There weren't even any drugs going around tonight, so I stood up and opened the front door to a male and female officer who both marched purposefully into the house.

'I'll take the upstairs,' the female officer said, heading towards the staircase. Kay now appeared at the top of the stairs, bare-chested.

'Stay where you are!' the female officer shouted at him, as she took the rest of the steps two at a time and started going through the rooms. The male police officer told me and Angela to stay downstairs while he questioned the men on the sofa in the living room, but they didn't seem to understand his questions and just stared at him blankly. After a minute or so he gave up.

A few moments later, the female officer came back downstairs holding Kay by the shoulder; he was naked from the waist up and had his hands cuffed behind his back. He looked really cross about the whole thing and kept asking her to take the cuffs off him.

'Sit down!' she ordered, directing him to the sofa, and he took a seat while a sheepish-looking Simone crept in behind them both, zipping up her jean shorts. Me and Angela looked at each other, stunned. We'd sobered up pretty quickly but the whole thing was just bizarre.

The male officer continued to question the men in the living room while the female officer took me, Simone and Angela through to the kitchen. She asked us all our names and our ages, which we told her, then she asked us what we were doing in this house with these older guys. The way she spoke to us, it felt like we had done something really bad.

'But we haven't done anything,' I insisted. 'We were just sitting here, having a drink.'

'I think you were doing more than just having a drink, Simone,' she said pointedly at my friend. 'What were you doing in the upstairs bedroom with a man nearly twice your age?'

Simone gazed blankly at the police officer and swayed gently. 'I dunno whatcha mean,' she slurred.

'I mean, that man is far too old for you,' the police officer sighed. 'You are fifteen – a minor. He's an adult, and if he did anything to you sexually, well, that could be a criminal offence.'

Simone just stared at her.

'Is there anything you want to tell me, Simone?' the officer asked.

Simone just pursed her lips and shook her head.

'No? Are you sure?' the female officer asked again.

'I don't think he should be in handcuffs,' Simone said, then hiccupped loudly. I giggled. 'He's not done anything wrong,' she went on. 'I mean, what's he done? We were just talking, that's all. Just chilling out and chatting and stuff.'

The policewoman stared at her for a while longer. 'You were chilling out and chatting and stuff . . . is that what you're telling me?'

'Yup!'

'Without your clothes on, Simone? Just chatting without your clothes on?' She clearly didn't believe a word of it but Simone stuck out her bottom lip and nodded.

'Mm-hmm. Just chatting.'

The policewoman sighed and told Simone to sit down because it looked like she might fall over if she stayed on her feet any longer. I really didn't know what the hell was going on. It was all very confusing. The policewoman went through to the lounge and talked quietly with the policeman. Then she went back into the lounge and took the cuffs off Kay.

'Okay, guys, party's over,' she said, as she walked back into the kitchen. Her radio blared loudly from her shoulder and I wondered why they had bothered to come here in the first place. 'Get your things together, we're taking you home.'

I started to gather my things and so did the others. Kay now had his top back on and was standing in the lounge with the three other guys, silently watching as we gathered up our bags and phones. I spied the bottle of vodka – there was still a little left in the bottom. *Should I grab it and put it in my bag?* The policeman was watching me. *Probably not.*

'You fellas have been warned,' the policeman said before we left the room. 'You have two minors in this house – children, under the age of consent. These children do not live here and appear to be completely intoxicated. On this occasion we're going to let you off with a warning but we'd better not find ourselves back here again or you'll be charged.'

The men all nodded and I turned to the policewoman, confused.

'Two minors? Who is that?'

'That's you and your friend Simone. Angela is sixteen so she's no longer considered a minor.'

We walked out into the street and the policeman said to get in the car because they were taking us home. For some reason, Angela had to walk back, which didn't seem fair to me. After all, we were all together, but the policeman said since she was over sixteen she wasn't a child, so they had no obligation to take her.

'So how's she meant to get home?' I asked.

'She can walk,' said the policeman. 'We're not a taxi service, you know!'

Simone told Angela to meet her back at her house, since it was far too late for her to try to get back to Huddersfield. I waved to her as we pulled away and headed back home. It had been a really weird night, all in all. Really weird. At least Dad wasn't home to see me getting a lift home in a cop car. He'd kill me!

'You know, you girls really ought to be more careful about the kind of people you hang out with.' The female police officer addressed us both from the front seat as the car rolled through the quiet streets. Simone and I exchanged eye-rolls. *Who was she to tell us who we should or shouldn't hang out with!*

'Those men aren't your friends,' she went on. 'You may think they are but they're not. They are just interested in one thing and that's getting you into the bedroom. Do you understand? This is a matter of your personal safety.' On and on she went. I wasn't listening. What did she know?

6.

Ways to Get High

IT WASN'T A GOOD day for me when Dad moved back home. For one thing, he brought his girlfriend Rose with him but, worse, she brought her teenage son Greg too and Dad gave him my room.

'You can share with your sister,' he told me when I walked back into the house to find all my stuff had been moved out of my room and plonked in the corridor upstairs.

'But Thea's there!' I objected. I really didn't want to share a room with my sister and her girlfriend.

'It's my bloody house and you'll do what you're told,' Dad snarled. 'Or so help me, I'll give you what for. And I'll tell you something else: you're going to start going to school, Caz, or there'll be trouble. I've been sent five fucking fines because of your truanting.'

I didn't really care about school. Frankly, when I was there I was mostly high so I didn't understand what was going on in the lessons. Getting high was all I really cared about. I hated being straight so much these days that I didn't even bother going into school unless I'd taken something. I'd wake up, roll myself a joint and then smoke half of it before I got myself ready. Then, once I felt the dope taking effect, calming me down, stopping the palpitations of my heart, I could function properly. I'd have a quick shower, get dressed and then walk to the bus stop. Once I was out of the house, I'd usually smoke the other half of the joint. Then I was ready for school.

But if I didn't have anything to smoke, I wouldn't get out of bed at all. So I was always careful to put something aside from the night before. No matter how off my face I was, I remembered to leave myself something to smoke before school. On a good day, I'd also have some fet, a pill or a little coke before school too. This was my routine now and I didn't appreciate Dad moving back into the house to mess things up. Dad's girlfriend Rose was alright, I suppose, but it annoyed me how much attention Dad paid to Greg when he wasn't even his own kid. Greg was a year younger than me and he went to a different school on the other side of town, so I didn't see him all that much. But now that we were all under the same roof, I noticed that he spent a lot of time with my dad – the pair of them were always out together, at the football, swimming or clothes shopping.

What was so great about Greg? It wasn't fair. The only time Dad even looked at me was to tell me off or whack me. He never took me to a footy match or bought me any clothes. If I wanted anything for myself I had to steal it. I stole my perfume and make-up from Asda, my clothes and shoes from River Island, New Look and TK Maxx, and I stole a lovely grey handbag from M&S. I'd been caught a few times over the years but the security guards usually let me off with a warning because I apologised and told them I wouldn't do it again. The one time it didn't work was in Wilko's, when I was caught for stealing make-up and blank CDs. The manager called the police and I was held in a cell for a little time before they let me go with a warning – once I'd promised that I wouldn't do it again. Well, I didn't steal from Wilko's again but I carried on stealing on a daily basis because I really didn't have any choice. I didn't know any other way of getting what I needed. One time I walked out of Asda with five bottles of vodka under a very large coat and nobody batted an eyelid. In the end, though, the Asda security guard caught me so many times I was banned from entering the store altogether.

In November 2009, me and Tammy caught the train to Bradford, where she sat her driving theory test. Standing outside the test centre, waiting for her, I lit up a fag and checked my messages. There were so many guys with my number now that I couldn't always tell who they were when they texted me. Suddenly a very large Asian guy sauntered up to me, smiling, and asked me what I was doing. He looked like he was in his mid-twenties. He was very chatty and told me his name was Fergy. When I told him my name, he said he hadn't seen me around before and asked if I was local to the area.

'Nah, I've come over from Halifax with my sister,' I said.

'Do you want to come out for a drink some time?'

'Erm, I suppose . . .' I was a little uncertain. Bradford wasn't my town. 'I'm going back to Halifax today.'

'Yeah, but it's not far. Just get on the train and I'll pick you up from the station,' Fergy instructed. 'Look, give me your number and I'll call you.'

So Fergy took my number and, a couple of days later, he invited me to Bradford for a night out. It was quite exciting – my first ever time going on the train by myself for the short journey from Halifax to Bradford. I felt very grown up as I boarded the train later that evening and, just as he promised, Fergy picked me up from the station. His friend drove us because, according to Fergy, he was banned for a while. Fergy said we were all going back to his friend's house for a drink and a chill. We pulled up at a three-storey house where there were several other guys and a white girl who appeared to be wearing a scarf around her head like Muslim girls do. I wondered if maybe she too had converted. We all went to the shop together and bought some booze then returned to the house. I hung back as Fergy opened the gates – I didn't like the look of the two Rottweilers in the backyard, even though they were chained to the wall.

'Don't worry about the dogs,' he laughed. 'They're not going to hurt you. They do exactly what I say.'

Inside, the house seemed strange because there appeared to be living rooms on different floors and lots of bathrooms and bedrooms. We stayed in the second-floor living room at first, drinking and smoking pot, until Fergy said to me, 'Come on,' and he took my arm and led me out of the living room and up the stairs. I was a little woozy from the booze and the dope but I didn't feel scared. He seemed nice and friendly, so I didn't feel under threat until he led me into a bedroom, closed the door and locked it behind us. It was when I heard the lock snapping shut in its bolt that I realised something bad was about to happen. *He's locked the door. Why would he do that?*

Fear crept over my body, causing me to shiver. Fergy came towards me, a slow, menacing smile on his face, and I knew one thing for certain: I wasn't going to get out of there until he got what he wanted.

He took my clothes off and then forced me down on the bed, which wasn't actually a bed at all, just two mattresses piled on top of each other. He was so large I felt crushed under his huge frame. He didn't speak, never said a word – just carried on doing what he wanted. There was nothing I could do. Even if I could have got out from under him, the door was locked. He pinned me back on the bed and put himself inside me. He was so heavy I found it hard to breathe, and I just hoped it would be over soon so I could get up and leave. Finally, after what felt like forever, he rolled off me and stood up. I was so relieved to be able to breathe again, I just lay there panting for a second. Then Fergy stood up and made a phone call. He spoke a few words then, moments later, he unlocked the door and I saw three other guys standing there.

Oh no. Now I knew I was in trouble.

The men came in and they too locked the door behind them. There were four big blokes in the room and me. Trapped and afraid, I asked if I could leave, but nobody responded. Nobody spoke to me at all. Instead, they each took turns to unbuckle their trousers and climb on top of me.

'Please,' I sobbed. 'Please just let me go.' But they didn't listen and, anyway, they didn't seem to care. I wept silently as they laughed and talked to each other in their own language, just waiting for their friend to finish so that they could 'have a go' next. I have no idea how long it lasted, but it felt like it would never end. The tears rolled silently down my cheeks as, one after another, they used my body like a piece of meat. Finally, after they'd all had their fill, they let me get up and put my clothes back on. I wanted to run away but I couldn't if I tried. Even if I could somehow get past the two ferocious Rottweilers in the backyard, there was a six-foot-high fence surrounding the house and the only way in and out was through the large iron gates, which were firmly padlocked. Besides, I had no idea where I was. I wanted to go home. I needed to go home. So I begged Fergy to take me to the train station. It was late, I had to get up for school the next day. *Please, please, take me home . . .*

Finally, after nearly an hour, he agreed, and we got into his friend's car. When we were nearly at the station, he grabbed me by the cheeks and very quietly said, 'Did you like that? Eh? You white bitch. If you tell anyone, I will kill you.'

As soon as he let go I jumped out of the car and ran. I didn't care that we were only stopped at the lights. I couldn't be in that car a second longer. I ran and I didn't look behind me once. Now I stood shaking on the platform edge, praying for a train to come as quickly as possible to take me back to Halifax and hoping that he wouldn't come after me. *Fergy – that bastard!* My limbs and ribs ached from all his weight that had borne down on me. I felt pummelled, flattened, beaten down. Do they know? I wondered, stealing quick glances up and down the platform at the other passengers. It was early morning and there was a handful of men and women in smart suits on their way to work, reading their papers, pretending not to see me. *Did they know?* I felt panicky and paranoid. *Could they tell I had just been raped?*

I kept my head down, ashamed and disorientated, frightened Fergy would change his mind, suddenly appear and force me go back in the car with him. When the train arrived, I got in and tucked myself into a corner of the carriage. Then I got out my phone and looked at my face in the camera. *Oh, my God. What a mess! Who is this person? Who is this girl I'm staring at?* I hardly recognised myself. My cheeks were streaked and stained with black mascara from all the tears and my hair was a matted mess. I felt wrecked and so disgusted with myself. Why had I gone there? I knew now that I'd made a big mistake. He'd seemed so friendly. I thought he was genuine when he offered to take me out for a drink. I never imagined this would happen. And yet it did. IT DID. Maybe I was stupid, maybe I was just unlucky, but this kind of stuff had happened to me a lot. It was my fault, I knew that, because I shouldn't have put myself in that situation. I was so ashamed of myself. I recalled how excited and happy I'd felt a few hours earlier as I took my first ever train journey alone – how stupid I had been!

It had been the worst night of my life and I just wanted to forget it ever happened. Even if I did want to tell someone, which I didn't, because I felt so utterly ashamed of myself, nobody would believe me anyway, so I tried not to think about it. I got home in the early hours and fell gratefully asleep, making sure I still had some dope ready for when I woke up. I didn't want to recall the ugly things that had happened to me when I was out of it, so I took more drugs to cover the shame. It helped to numb my feelings and shield me from reality. And as the days and weeks passed by, I took more and more so that every day I got higher and higher. It wasn't enough now to wait for a drink in the afternoon. I'd usually have a drink or two during the school day too, just to get me through. I'd buy a bottle of Coke on the way into school, drink half of it and pour some vodka into the rest so I could swig on it throughout the day without attracting attention.

My home life seemed to have deteriorated since Dad moved back. I had no privacy any more, no peace, and whenever I walked through the front door, Dad seemed ready to greet me with a smart fist. So, at the beginning of 2010, I went to live with Marie. She'd just had a little boy, Adam, and she needed help looking after the two older kids – Dara and Samuel – while she coped with the baby. It was the perfect excuse to get away from Dad, and I suppose it was okay at first. I adored Dara and I would walk her to school each morning before taking myself to school. But I quickly saw that Marie was struggling because Ross was violent towards her. He smacked her once when the baby was in her arms and she fell into the TV, all because he couldn't get a decent signal. I saw him do some horrible things to her – pushing her down the stairs, smashing her head into a door and plenty more besides. She wanted to leave him, and she had succeeded a couple of times, but he always managed to track her down and persuade her to go back to him. Now, with another baby, I think she felt trapped. And she was too scared to report him to the police. I didn't know what to do except help by getting the kids out of the way whenever he was in a violent mood.

The thing was, it was also a very druggie house. My sister knew a dealer who could get pills for 45p each, and she liked to take fet too. She would get up in the morning, make a baby bottle for Sean, give Dara breakfast, then she'd build a fet bomb for each of us. Sometimes I would build the bomb but, either way, I would usually be coming up just as I was getting to school, so I was always too hyper and high to concentrate in my lessons. It didn't help with my sister's mental health either – she heard voices and I think the drugs made things much worse.

Most days I would be approached on the street by some guy in a car and I was always being called and texted to ask if I was going out. There were nights I really didn't want to go but I didn't feel like I could say no. When I told them I wasn't sure, they would go on and on at me, badgering me until I agreed. And if I persisted they would make some threatening comment about my little cousin Dara, saying they knew where she lived. Then I realised I had no choice. I would get in their cars, they'd give me a drink, a smoke, maybe something stronger and, before I knew it, I was in a hotel in Leeds, Huddersfield, Bradford or Manchester. Sex became something I started to expect. I guess it was the price I had to pay for the free drink and drugs. At some point I'd stagger home, usually in the early hours of the morning, or even halfway through the next day, and I either made it to school, or I didn't.

'Caz, where the fuck have you been?' my sister yelled one morning when I came in at 7 a.m., just as she was getting the kids up for school.

'Nowhere,' I slurred, heading wearily upstairs for my room. My head felt woolly from too many drugs.

'You can't treat this place like a hotel,' she shouted after me. 'What are you playing at? I thought you were going to take Dara to school this morning.'

'Sorry, can't,' I whispered, as I dragged myself into my bed.

'I'm getting sick of this, Caz,' she fumed. 'It's a fucking disgrace. You should be in school!' Maybe she said more but I wasn't sure, because I'd already crawled under my duvet and closed my eyes.

One time, my sister tried to stop me going out but I went anyway and she called my dad, who came out to find me. I didn't know he was after me until I saw his familiar outline running towards me as I stood in the park, talking to a guy.

'Cassie!' Dad yelled when he caught sight of me. 'Come here, you little runt!'

'Oh shit!' I got the shock of my life, so I took off, running out of the park and through the backstreets to get away from him. The only thing I knew for certain was that if Dad caught up with me he'd beat the crap out of me, so I ran, diving this way and that, to escape him.

In the end it was all too much for Marie and, in February 2010, she said she couldn't cope any more. My school attendance had dropped to thirty-seven per cent, I was out of control and she sent me back to Dad's house. There, he gave me a hiding, grabbing me round the throat and whacking me hard. That's when the authorities got involved again. They sent out a parent support worker, and when she asked how I got the marks on my neck, I told her the truth – that my dad had hit me for being out of control. The police were called and I told them I never wanted to live with my dad again. The problem was that my sister didn't want me either, so Social Services looked around for another family member I could live with.

That's when I went to live with Dad's sister Bernie. She was nice but she worked twelve-hour shifts in a care home while her daughter worked in a chip shop during the day and a bar at night, so there wasn't anyone home when I got in from school. I just carried on living the way I had before. I was there five weeks before she caught me stealing six pounds from her purse to buy fags and chucked me out. In May I went to live with her son Alan for a while, and that was alright. He was also into drugs, so we smoked a lot of dope and fet together and got high. But Social Services said it wasn't an appropriate place for me to live, and told me I had to go and live with Dad again. It was the last thing I wanted, but in mid-June 2010 I had run out of options and was forced to move back in with Dad. A new outreach worker was appointed to work with me and Dad, focusing on helping us get along, and they said we had to attend fifteen meetings together. I tried to get to most of them but Dad never showed up. I knew he wouldn't – he hated Social Services and said the sessions were a waste of his time.

Now I rarely bothered with school. What was the point? I didn't understand anything anyway. And with everything going on at home, getting high and all the blokes, it was just too much. But Dad insisted I went otherwise he'd get fined. So, most weekdays I got up, put on my uniform, got the bus to school, signed in the register and then walked straight out again. The only reason I bothered to turn up at all was because if Dad got fined he would go mental and beat the shit out of me. He said I was costing him a fortune in fines. Occasionally I got caught bunking off and I'd be given detention but there didn't seem to be much point keeping me in school. I wasn't learning anything there. The only thing I cared about these days was getting high.

7.

Tupac

BASTARD!

I watched the small silver car disappear down the country lane – away, out of view. *Bastard!* What was I meant to do now? Just a moment ago I'd been having a nice time with Sam and Jay, chatting, smoking joints. It had been Jay's idea to come out to the Yorkshire Dales for a drive and a smoke – a place far out of town because he was paranoid about getting stopped by the police in Halifax. Jay was around twenty-eight and Sam's boyfriend – at least, that's what she told me – and we were having a nice time, driving round the hilly, heather-covered moors, going past small villages and exploring the dips and valleys of the Dales. I loved it – I loved being out in the countryside. I loved the fresh country air and the wide, sweeping views of the hills. The only problem was I'd been drinking vodka and Coke and now I was desperate for a wee.

'Stop here, would you, Jay?' I pointed to a small layby.

'What for?'

'I need to get out and have a pee.'

They both laughed and Jay pulled in. I hopped out, scrambled down a small bank and hid behind a tree. Then, just as I was emerging, I heard Jay's engine starting up, and to my horror, the car pulled out of the layby and headed off down the road.

I stood watching it for a few seconds, too shocked to move. Was this a joke or did he really intend to leave me out there on my own, miles from Halifax? The silence of the countryside now crowded in on me as I realised that, either way, I didn't really have any choice – I had to walk. Calculating that I was at least an hour's walk from the last village we had passed through, I set off back down the road we had come from. *Bastard!* I cursed Jay under my breath as I trudged along the small, single-track road.

He probably thought it was funny, leaving me like that. Or maybe he was just keen to get Sam alone and didn't fancy taking me back to Halifax. Either way, it was a bloody nightmare. Even if I got to the next town I didn't have enough money for a cab home. I would probably have to walk back to Halifax, and how long would that take? Four, five hours, maybe? *For fuck's sake!* A couple of cars went by and I stopped to let them pass safely. The passengers all looked at me curiously, as if to say: *What's she doing out here in the middle of nowhere on her own?* I could understand their confusion – in my small skirt and denim jacket, I didn't look like the average Dales hiker.

After about twenty minutes, another car came down the road and, once again, I stopped to let them pass. But this car slowed down and, as it rolled up to where I was standing, the front passenger window wound down. A bald Asian man with a goatee, smoking a joint, addressed me: 'Hey! What are you doing?'

'Me? I'm going home.'

'Yeah, but why are you out here in the fields and stuff on your own?'

I peered into the car – there were four blokes. Two in the front and two in the back.

I shrugged.

'Where do you live?'

'Halifax.'

'Well, do you want a lift? We're going in that direction and you can't walk all the way back from here.'

'Yeah, sure,' I said.

'Hop in, then!'

On the way back, the guy who'd offered me a lift introduced himself as Tupac and asked me my name. They offered me the joint that was going round and I took a couple of puffs. They seemed OK, these guys, and I was certainly grateful for the lift back.

'You can drop me here,' I said, pointing to the corner of Queen Street, just before the turning that led to my road. I didn't want to invite unwelcome questions from Dad.

'What are you doing later?' asked Tupac. 'Do you want to go out for a drink and a chill?'

'Yeah, okay.' We exchanged numbers and Tupac said he would give me a call later.

'Where do you want me to pick you up from?' he asked.

'Just here,' I said. 'Where you're dropping me.'

Later that night I got a call from Tupac, who said he was in the area and would be at our meeting point in five minutes. I went to the corner to meet him and we drove to a corner shop to pick up some booze. Then we drove to a hotel in Bradford, where he bought a room for the night.

'Stay here,' he instructed, as he got out of the car. 'I'll get the key from reception first and then I'll come back and give it to you. We can't go in together. It won't look good.'

I knew what he meant. I was pretty young to be going into hotel rooms with older guys and it was a bit risky if the night manager saw us go up together. I'd been in this situation before – when one of the guys had gone in first to buy the room and I'd been told to wait in the car out of sight – except on those previous occasions the guy had actually locked the car door before going into the hotel first! To stop me jumping out, I suppose. But Tupac didn't lock the car door and I was pleased that he trusted me. I watched him approach the reception and saw the young man behind the desk hand over the keycard.

Tupac came back to the car and gave me the keycard. 'Room three-four-four. It's on the third floor. You got up first and I'll join you in a few minutes,' he said.

I nodded, took the card and walked through the reception without giving the manager a second glance. I found the room easily. It was a typical, nondescript hotel room – bland beige walls, blue curtains, prints of flowers. I used the toilet, put the TV on and waited for Tupac. A few minutes later, there was a knock on the door.

'It's me,' he whispered. I opened up and he came in carrying blue plastic bags full of vodka and Coke. We smiled at each other conspiratorially, then he took off his coat, sat down on the bed and rolled a joint. After an hour or so, he fished around in his jacket pocket and pulled out a small bag of white powder.

'It's coke,' he said. 'Wanna do a line?'

'Sure,' I said.

As he poured the powder onto the small coffee table and chopped it expertly with his credit card, Tupac asked me why I had been out in the Dales on my own. I explained about going for a drive with Sam and Jay, and how he'd driven off when I got out to go for a wee. Tupac laughed as I described the moment of watching the car roar off down the road, leaving me alone in the middle of nowhere.

'It's not funny,' I said, though I could feel a hint of a smile playing on my lips as he guffawed loudly.

'It's pretty funny,' he insisted. 'You've got to admit.'

I looked down and, slowly, I let the grin escape. 'Yeah, well, it wouldn't have been funny at all if you hadn't stopped to give me a lift. I don't think I'd be laughing if I had to walk home.'

'You'd still be walking now!' he erupted, and we both cracked up. Tupac seemed like a good guy and we did a few more lines together before he made his move. I didn't mind so much with him – at least he was nice to me and talked to me like a human being. He dropped me home the next morning and, before I got out, he took my face in his hands and kissed me on the lips.

'I'll call you soon, okay?' he said.

'Yeah.'

'Look after yourself, Caz,' he grinned. 'No more trips to the Dales!'

'No way,' I agreed. 'If I see that Jay again . . .'

'If you see him, you make sure you call me and I'll come round and break his knees. Okay?'

I laughed. I liked Tupac.

We met up a few more times after that, and the pattern was always the same. He'd pick me up and then take me to the same hotel in Bradford for a drink, a smoke and a chill. We'd talk for hours and hours, me and Tupac. It wasn't like the times with so many of the other guys, who just wanted to have sex and nothing else. Tupac told me about his life – he was thirty and dealing drugs, but he said he didn't want to do it for ever. He wanted to get clean so he could be a better dad for his little girl. But right now he was on bail for a drug dealing offence and there was a strong chance he could go to prison for it.

I told him about my mum and how she had died from Huntington's disease. I told him about my dad too, and how he beat me up. With Tupac, I didn't just put up with the sex; I felt like he really cared. In the early hours of the morning he said things to me no other guy had said before. He told me he loved me and that I was his girlfriend. He said he'd never felt like this with anyone before and he wanted to be with me. He even said he wanted to have a baby with me one day. He seemed genuine, like he had these very strong feelings for me, and the more he talked about those feelings, the more I liked him. I cared about him and I felt he cared for me too. As the sun came up, we'd get dressed and he'd take me home again. It felt like Tupac and I were close.

Meanwhile, at home, things were as bad as they had ever been. Dad had taken to locking me out of the house if I came home beyond his curfew. He said I couldn't just waltz in any time I liked and that he was sick of being woken up at all hours of the morning. The first couple of times he locked me out, I'd thrown a stone up at Tammy's window and she had come down to let me in. But then, one time in late November 2010, I walked into the house and Dad came flying off the sofa and pushed me back out again.

'But it's eleven o'clock,' I cried, as I staggered back onto the street. He slammed the door after me and I stood there as light flurries of snow fell on the pavement.

'It's eleven thirty-five' he yelled back through the door.

'Eleven thirty-five? It's not even that late,' I replied. 'What am I meant to do? I'm gonna freeze out here!'

'Tough shit,' he shouted back. 'You should have thought of that before you decided to ignore your curfew. If you can't come in at a decent time, don't fucking bother coming home at all.'

I didn't even have a coat. I pulled my cardigan around myself tightly and sat down on the front step, the cold hard paving slab numbing my behind. I knew it was pointless arguing with him. Once he'd made up his mind, he never backed down. I couldn't even call Tammy because she was working nights that week at the packing factory. So I sat and shivered.

After about ten minutes I heard the window opening above me and I looked up. Dad leant out of the window and, for a moment, my heart lifted. *He's changed his mind! He's going to let me back in the house again.*

'Mind your head,' he shouted. And a lighter came spinning down from where he had dropped it, quickly followed by a cigarette.

'That's all you're getting from me tonight!' he shouted.

Oh, thanks a fucking lot! I thought, as I took the cigarette and lighter and walked off down the street. *I had better find a car to get into. I really don't have much choice.*

The only time Dad was forced to let me in was when the police picked me up for being a missing person or drunk and disorderly. Then they'd put me in the police car and drive me home. I really didn't want to go back, knowing it would put Dad in a terrible mood. 'He's gonna hit me,' I told them flatly. 'The moment you walk off, he's going to beat the crap out of me.' But they didn't care. They had to take me back, they said, because he was my dad.

One night, Tupac picked me up and we went to our usual hotel for a drink and some lines of coke. I really liked coke because it meant I could drink and smoke loads and I didn't feel too out of it. It was weird – it got you high and sober at the same time. And because Tupac was a dealer he always had loads of the stuff and he never asked me to pay for it.

'That's my brother,' Tupac said, as his mobile rang. He answered the phone and started chatting away in a combination of English and Urdu. Then, after he finished the call, he said his brother and some friends were on their way over. 'They'll have to get another room though,' he said, as he rolled up a twenty-pound note, preparing to snort another line. 'We can't all stay in here. It's four to a room, max.'

Tupac and I had some more coke and ended up having sex. Afterwards he got a message on his phone. 'They're in the next room,' he said.

A second later there was a knock on the door and six people piled in. I was still in bed, naked, so I hurriedly pulled the covers over me as four Asian men and two white girls, roughly the same age as me, walked in. I was surprised to see so many people in the room – they brought booze with them and suddenly there was a party atmosphere. Lots of noise, booze, more lines of coke, and the guys were all laughing and talking in their own language.

'Who's this, then?' Tupac asked the guys, nodding to the girls.

'Couple of nice girls we just picked up off the kerb,' answered another guy and they all laughed. None of the blokes spoke to me except the guy who had told Tupac that he'd picked the girls up from the street, who leant towards me and seemed to be saying something with an angry voice.

'What's going on?' I wanted to say, but the words had barely formed in my mouth before I felt a sharp stinging sensation on my cheek. It took a few seconds to register what had happened. My hand flew to my face as the raw pain spread from my jaw up my cheek. *He had hit me! One of the men had come straight up to me and slapped me in the face.*

'Shut up, you stupid white bitch!' he shouted angrily, as I recoiled from the attack. *Who was this man? What was he doing here?* I looked to Tupac for help but he just carried on smoking a joint. He didn't say a word. I scrambled towards the headboard and curled into a ball. Seeing my fear, the strange man started to laugh.

He was Asian, like the others, but he wore two large sovereign rings on his fingers and had a big gold chain round his neck.

'Look at her!' he said. He pointed at me, said something in his own language, and the others started to laugh too.

'What did you do that for?' I sniffed quietly, and the guy lifted his hand once more in a threatening way. The rings glinted dangerously in the light of the bedside lamp.

'You better keep your mouth shut or I'll do it again, bitch!' he snapped. The others laughed again. *Yeah, I thought to myself. Beating up a girl half your size. You're really the big man.*

I couldn't help myself – I didn't want to, but I started to cry. 'Please, please take me home,' I whispered to Tupac. 'I want to go home.' But Tupac wasn't listening. 'Please,' I said, a little louder this time. 'Please take me home, Tupac.'

Tupac looked over at me, as if seeing me for the first time. 'Ah no, you're alright,' he said, picking up a cup with vodka in it and passing it to me. 'Stay and have a drink. Look, I'm just about to make some lines. Come on, stay and have them with me.'

So I stayed. I really didn't have any choice. The others left the room and Tupac got up to see them out, locking the door behind him. I wasn't comfortable. I really just wanted to go home. I started to get dressed. Tupac went over to the desk and chopped out another line of coke.

'What are you doing?' he said.

'Getting dressed. I wanna go home,' I said. 'Can you please take me home now?'

'Don't be silly. Just have another line.' He snorted his line then held out the rolled-up twenty-pound note. I didn't feel like it, but I did it. Then I sat down on the bed, feeling hopeless. I didn't know where I was and, besides that, I had no money to get back. I needed Tupac to take me home.

Tupac came up behind me and started kissing my neck. 'Come on, relax, Cassie,' he murmured, unhooking my bra and pulling down my top. 'You're beautiful,' he said, as he pushed me back down on the bed.

'I just want to go home, Tupac,' I said again. I felt his hands crawling up and down my body but I didn't like it. I didn't feel good about what was happening. 'Please,' I said softly, turning my face away. 'Please don't. I don't want to have sex with you now.'

'Shhh,' he whispered, as he climbed on top of me. 'Just go with it, Cassie. Come on.'

He wouldn't take no for an answer and there was nothing I could do to stop him. He had sex with me and then, afterwards, he took another line and went next door. That's when the four other guys came in. I saw one of them had pulled the door bolt across. I knew what was coming and that's when I grabbed the bottle of vodka from the bedside table and took a long, deep swig. If they were coming for me, I just wanted to be out of it.

They all took turns, one by one, and between men I tried to glug down as much vodka as I could. A joint came round, I inhaled deeply, and then again. And again. Eventually I lost consciousness, and sometime in the early hours I came round enough to see that there were two other girls in the room. There was more booze, more cannabis, and more coke. Every time I came round there was somebody different in the room. I could hear them talking loudly in their own language – talking and laughing together – but no one spoke to me. My stomach lurched, I felt sick but I didn't throw up. I just took another line.

What's going on? Who are these people? Where's Tupac?

It was so strange and confusing. There were all these people coming and going. I blacked out several times. The next thing I knew, I woke up and Tupac was in the room.

'Come on,' he said. 'Let's get you home.'

I sat up and, like a zombie, I pulled all my clothes back on, not saying a word. Then we got into Tupac's car and he drove me back to Halifax. I was silent the whole way home. I couldn't have spoken even if I'd wanted to, which I didn't. I was numb and dumb. When I got out of the car he said, 'See you soon, Caz.' But I didn't respond. What was there to say?

A couple of weeks later, Tupac messaged me to ask me if I was alright. It was the first time I'd heard from him since *that night.*

'Yeah, fine,' I replied.

'Sorry 4 my brother and his friends,' he wrote. 'Hope u r ok. No hard feelings. OK?'

For a second my thumb hovered over the delete button. Then I sighed. 'OK,' I replied.

And there were no hard feelings, I guess. None. No feelings at all.

On the day he was due to appear in court, Tupac called and asked if I wanted to spend some time with him. I agreed and he took me to our usual hotel. He lit a joint, took a drag and handed it to me.

'I think I'm going down today,' he sighed. 'My lawyer says I should expect a custodial sentence. That means prison. So, I . . .

erm . . . I just wanted to say sorry for what happened – you know, with the guys the other night. I didn't want them to hurt you but there was nothing I could have done.'

He paused and I said, 'It's alright. Are you really going to prison today?'

He nodded. 'I'll write to you while I'm away. Will you write to me?'

'Yeah, sure.'

'I love you, Caz. You have to wait for me, okay?'

I nodded and then he got up and took his coat into the bathroom. He was in there for ages and I was just starting to wonder whether to go and check on him when he came out, carrying five small sausage-shaped packages, twisted tight at both ends, in a hotel bath towel.

'What's that?' I asked, as he placed them on the bed.

'That is heroin, coke and weed. I have to make sure they're wrapped really tight before I take them inside with me. I've got to do it now.' He then disappeared into the bathroom again, and when he came back out he was no longer carrying the packages.

'Done it,' he grimaced. 'Come on, let's go.'

Tupac was true to his word. He was sent down for five years and he wrote to me from prison – heartfelt, loving letters full of emotion – saying how much he missed me and cared about me. I didn't reply to any of them. It was only many years later that I realised that Tupac coming to pick me up from the Dales was no coincidence. Like a drug deal, I had been dropped off and picked up again. I had been handed over.

8.

Pete

WHAT AM I GOING to do?

The question kept swirling around and around in my head and I didn't have an answer. My life seemed to have gone from bad to terrible in the last month. In November I was arrested for shoplifting and the police took me to the station and tested me for drugs. They found cocaine in my system and I was given a juvenile reprimand. Then, about a week later, I found out I was pregnant. I knew my periods weren't regular but missing two periods was unusual, even for me. Just to be on the safe side I did a home test and was horrified when it came out positive. I knew in my heart this was a possibility – after all, none of the men I went with ever used protection – still, I never thought it would happen to me. Now I was overwhelmed with fear. What the hell was I going to do? I couldn't tell anybody, let alone my dad, so I just tried to forget about it and pretend it wasn't happening.

But of course, it didn't just go away on its own, and after a while my school skirt started getting tight. Then my teacher noticed the small bump and she asked me outright if I was pregnant. I didn't see any point in lying.

'Cassie – is there someone at home we can talk to?' she asked. 'Should we call your dad?'

'NO!' I said forcefully. 'No, don't call my dad. I don't want him to know.'

'Well, at least we have to let your GP know so that you can get proper health checks.'

'I suppose so . . .' I said reluctantly.

I was in a fog of confusion. I was fifteen years old and terrified that if I went to the doctors they would tell my dad. Who could I turn to for help? I didn't know. One night, it all came spilling out of me when I was in a car with a guy I knew. I confided that I was pregnant but I didn't know what to do. A few days later a man pulled up next to me in a black car while I was walking home from school. It was someone I'd never seen before.

'Are you Cassie?' he asked.

'How do you know my name?'

'Through a friend. So . . . do you want to go for a smoke?'

I got in the car and we pulled up in a deserted car park on the outskirts of town. He said his name was Mo and, like so many of the guys who approached me, he seemed really friendly. He chatted while he rolled a joint. Then he lit it, took a couple of puffs and passed it to me. I took a long drag and, after I'd exhaled, he asked me, 'Are you pregnant?'

'Yes, but I don't want to be.'

'I can help you,' he said. 'I can help arrange a termination for you. Do you want me to help you?'

I thought about it for a second. This was probably the best way. I didn't want the baby and I knew my dad would kill me if he ever found out. If this man could help arrange things quietly then perhaps my dad would never need to know. 'Okay,' I said. 'Yes.'

I barely knew this man. He was a stranger to me but, because he knew my friend, I decided that he could be trusted. What choice did I have? I felt the small life growing inside me and I felt nothing but horror and shame. The drugs were my only escape from the grim reality of my situation, but each morning I woke up and my head was clear again. And once more the truth came rushing at me, making me sick with fear.

In early December Mo picked me up to take me to an appoint-ment at a clinic some way from my home. I explained my situation and they agreed not to tell my dad – they said that since this was a private clinic, it didn't have to go on my NHS record. Then, after a lengthy consultation, they agreed to give me the pills for a medical abortion. Mo then drove me back to a house in Halifax where I had to go through the process of 'passing the foetus'.

When it happened, it was the most horrible moment of my life. I saw it! I actually saw the tiny, bloodied body with my own eyes and then, a moment later, I flushed the toilet and it was gone. I collapsed onto the floor of the bathroom as the pain engulfed me completely. I felt more alone than ever before. My stomach ached with emptiness, my insides twisted and groaned. I was weak, tired and full of pain – but I felt I deserved nothing less. All those fancy words they used in the clinic like 'termination', 'abortion', 'procedure' and 'foetus' couldn't hide the fact that I had killed my baby. I was full of shame. And guilt. Overwhelming, inescapable guilt. *What right did I have to take another human life?* It had been my child, my innocent child growing inside me, and now it was gone. I wanted to weep but there were no tears inside and no one to put their arm around me and hold me. All I wanted was to curl up, go to sleep and never wake up again. Instead, I went downstairs and asked Mo if he had some dope. If I couldn't cry, at least I could try to forget.

I stayed in that house for five days, recovering from the termination and smoking dope to get through the pain, both physical and mental. Waves of cramps kept me pinned to the bed while sadness and shock drained all my energy. I'd had no idea what to expect, but nobody said it would feel so bad. And though I knew I didn't have any choice, I was full of regret at what I had done. Now that the baby was no longer inside me, I tortured myself by thinking about their life. I wondered whether it would have been a boy or a girl. I thought about when he or she would have been born and imagined how I would have enjoyed being a mum. It was hell, every moment.

Eventually I was well enough to return home, where I told Dad I'd been staying with a friend. I didn't tell him about the pregnancy – I didn't tell anyone. He didn't seem bothered that I'd been away. It was now the Christmas holidays, so it didn't matter if I was out for several nights at a time. Dad really didn't care if I was at home or not. The only thing he cared about was getting fined if I was out of school.

Once the new term started I carried on back at school as if nothing had happened. 'What about the baby?' my teacher asked one afternoon in January.

'I got rid of it,' I told her blankly. And that was that. Only it didn't feel like nothing had happened. I felt worse than I had in my entire life. All I wanted to do was forget, so I smoked and drank more and that made it all go away. I missed school sometimes but I didn't care – at least not until Dad had been issued with another fine.

On 7 February 2011 I marched into school seething, my lip throbbing with pain. I hated my dad, hated him! I couldn't believe what he'd done. I kept my head low and my eyes down. I didn't want to see anyone that day. I'd only had one small joint that morning and I wasn't in a good mood. I signed myself in and then went into my first lesson of the day – English. But I'd barely sat down before the teacher approached me.

'Cassie? Are you okay? Your lip is very swollen.'

I shrugged.

'Come on, let's get you to the school counsellor. Come on, come with me.' The teacher took me out of the classroom and walked me through to the school office, where I noted the concerned faces on the members of the admin staff. The lovely school counsellor, Jill, sat me down in her office with a cup of tea. She talked to me with kindness and sympathy, and it caught me off guard. I felt a lump in my throat.

'Cassie, how did you get that nasty-looking bruise on your lip?' she asked eventually.

I didn't see the point of hiding the truth. 'It was my dad,'

I said, wincing with pain. 'He hit me on the stairs and then I fell down them.'

The counsellor's eyes widened in shock and I took a sip of my tea. *Ouch!* The hot water stung when it reached my upper lip. I thought back to the night before when I had come in from a night out, intending to go straight upstairs to my room. But I'd met Dad on the landing and he seemed really pissed off with me. Even more than usual.

'I've got another one of them bloody letters!' he bellowed furiously. 'What do you think you're playing at, Caz?'

I didn't reply and this seemed to make him angrier. He took a step towards me and gave me a big, open-handed slap across the face. It was such a forceful blow, my head ricocheted off the wall and I toppled backwards down the stairs. I landed awkwardly on the bottom with a heavy thud and lay there for a few seconds, dazed.

'You're a fucking waste of space, Cassie Pike,' Dad yelled from the top of the stairs. 'You've given me nothing but fucking trouble. And I've had it up to here!'

I lay there sobbing for a while, holding my bleeding lip. Then, eventually, I managed to crawl back to the bedroom I shared with Tammy and Thea. I looked at myself in the mirror, dabbing at the cut with a damp tissue. Already I could see my lip swelling, and by morning it was three times its normal size and a blueish-black colour.

Fuck it, I thought, as I took another sip of sweet milky tea in Jill's office. *I'm not going to lie to protect him.* So I told Jill exactly what happened and she nodded sympathetically, her head cocked to one side, her brow knitted with worry. Then, as my tears threatened to spill over, she passed me a box of tissues, got up and said she needed to have a word with the Head. She closed the door behind her, and for a few minutes I listened as Jill engaged the Headteacher in a hushed conversation. All I could hear were little snippets through the door – words like 'abusive', 'call the police' and 'Social Services'. More trouble, I thought. Dad wasn't going to be happy about that but I really didn't care any more. I didn't care about anything.

Then I saw the uniformed officers enter the school office and I knew they were there to question me about my lip. Pete was one of the officers. I had met Pete a few days earlier after Rose had reported me missing. He was the Missing Person's Coordinator for the police. After I'd found my way home again, he had come to our house and sat me down to explain that I was at 'high risk of harm' because I was a young person and I'd been seen getting in and out of older men's cars. I liked Pete from the start – he talked to me like I was a human being; he didn't talk down to me or give me a hard time. Of medium height and with short brown hair, Pete had a kind face and large, soft brown eyes. He explained that because I was out all hours of the day and night, and because of my regular drinking and drug use, I was considered a 'vulnerable person'. And although he couldn't stop me doing anything, he wanted me to know that I could call him anytime from anywhere. Then he handed me his card and, with a very serious look, he said: 'Cassie, I want to help you. I want you to be safe. Can you promise me something?'

I was silent. I wasn't going to agree to anything before I knew what it was.

He sighed. 'Just promise that you'll call if you're ever in trouble. Call me. I won't judge you. I won't be angry. I'll just come and get you. Okay?'

I nodded.

Now I told Pete and the other officer about how my dad had whacked me the day before, giving me a busted lip. They scribbled in their notebooks and asked a few questions.

'Are you going to arrest him?' I asked before they left. 'Will he go to prison?'

'We'll make enquiries,' Pete replied. 'That's all I can say at this stage.'

'You should lock him up,' I insisted. 'He deserves to be in prison, that bastard!'

'We'll see.'

I worried all that day about what would happen when I got home. Would they take him down the police station? Would he be angry with me for ratting on him? In the end I needn't have worried at all because, as far as I knew, nothing ever happened.

Life was pretty chaotic for me after that. I saw Pete every now and again. Occasionally he called to ask me where I was when my dad or Rose reported me as a missing person. Then there were the times he turned up out of the blue. He'd ask me questions and I'd tell him a little but not too much.

Do I have a boyfriend?

No.

Do you drink much?

About four bottles of vodka a week.

Do you take drugs?

Sometimes I smoke weed. Sometimes I take pills.

That was it – he'd nod, make his notes and go away again.

One night, at the end of March 2011, I came in from a night out and Dad was waiting for me in the lounge, holding one of my mobile phones.

'I've been going through your phone,' he said with a look of disgust. 'I can't believe the stuff I've been reading. There's sick messages from all sorts of men. Sick, perverted messages. Who are they? Who are these blokes? Ten, twenty of them . . . they can't all be your boyfriend.'

I didn't reply.

'You're a disgrace, Caz, a fucking disgrace.'

'No, I'm not,' I shot back angrily. I wasn't going to let him say that about me. 'How can you say that?'

'Me?' he erupted. 'It's you! You slut. What have you been doing?'

'What do you care?' I shouted back. 'Stay out of my phone. Stay out of my life. I hate you.'

'Cassie!' Rose shouted at me. 'Calm down. Your father's just looking out for you.'

'Rubbish. He doesn't give a shit. He's only out for himself. I hate him.'

Dad swung for me but I ducked and picked up the first thing that came to hand – a small vase – and threw it at him. It crashed into the wall.

'I'm calling the police!' Rose screeched. 'Cassie! I'm calling the police!'

The police came and I was arrested for being drunk and disorderly and thrown in the cells to 'sober up'. I thought it was a bit rich, frankly. After all, Dad was always the one who was beating up on me and the police knew it. Why did they always take his side? I couldn't work it out. Pete seemed apologetic as he handed me a rough woollen blanket and a thin, lumpy pillow.

'Just get some rest, Cassie,' he said. 'We're not keeping you here because you've done anything wrong. We're just trying to prevent a breach of the peace. Also, it looks like you could do with some sleep.'

I thought it would take me ages to fall asleep on the hard cell mattress, but not long after I lay down and closed my eyes, I passed out.

I was woken the next morning by a banging on the cell door.

'Wake up, Cassie.' The duty officer came in with a cup of tea and some toast. I thought I would be let out but after a couple of hours Pete came into my cell and said there had been a new, unrelated allegation made against me that morning and they couldn't let me out. Instead they were re-arresting me.

'What?' I was outraged. 'What for?'

'We've had a report from a girl who says she's a friend of yours – Janine Dooley. We've taken a statement this morning and, consequently, we are arresting and interviewing you on suspicion of facilitating a child sexual offence.'

'What? What the hell is that meant to mean? I don't know what you're talking about.'

Pete said they would explain everything in the interview room. So I waited in the cell until they were ready to interview me and then, late on Saturday afternoon, they took me into a little room where they explained what Janine had said. I knew Janine quite well – we were distant cousins and had been friends for about five years. Pete read the statement in a flat, emotionless voice while I struggled to make sense of her words.

'"Cassie Pike tricked me into getting into a car with two unknown Asian men. I was taken to a restaurant in Huddersfield where I was sexually assaulted before being taken home."'

Pete put the statement down on the desk and looked at me, questioningly. 'Does this statement ring any bells?'

I sighed. I knew the exact day she was talking about, and I started to get angry.

'Yes, I know Janine,' I said crossly. 'That's the only time we've ever been in a car together. Basically, we missed the school bus and neither of us had any money to get back. So I used her phone to call a friend to give us a lift. Two guys I know picked us up and we had a joint on the way back to my house. Then they dropped us off round the corner from my home. Except Janine never got out. The blokes we were with offered to take her out and buy her a meal and she agreed. I actually told her to get out of the car but she wouldn't. What could I do? She kept saying she was alright and not to worry because she was fine. So I left and that was that. I messaged her later to check she'd got home okay but she never replied.'

It was the two Imies who had given us the lift that night, and I did try to get Janine to come with me because I wasn't sure they would be good to her. But I couldn't force her.

'In her statement Janine says she was sexually assaulted before being taken home,' Pete read. 'Were you in the car when that happened?'

'No! I just told you – when I was in the car nothing happened at all. Then they dropped me off and I don't know what happened after that. It was her choice to stay in the car. What could I do? I told her to get out of the car with me.'

This questioning went on for some time and the whole thing felt very unfair. After all, if a man had assaulted her it was hardly my fault! They tried to get me to describe Imie 1 and Imie 2, and I did my best. I didn't tell them of course about what Imie 2 had done to me – that was all in the past, anyway. I was held in the cells on Saturday and Sunday night while they made further enquiries and then, finally, they let me go on Monday morning without charge.

'We can't identify the perpetrator of the alleged assault, nor can we link you to it,' Pete explained as he filled out my release forms.

'Yeah, because I haven't done anything wrong,' I said under my breath, for what felt like the hundredth time. 'I'm not a criminal, you know.'

Pete sighed. 'I know you're not, Cassie. We're just doing our job, following up on a serious criminal allegation.'

I saw Pete a few times after that – he picked me up once or twice when I was reported missing – and one day in April he came to the door because my dad had gone through my phone again and found 'dirty messages'. Dad accused me of being a prostitute. I didn't know what he was talking about – a prostitute gets paid for having sex and I never got paid. I just went out with loads of different guys and sometimes it ended up with sex. One time, the guy had even asked *me* for money!

His name was Big Maj and, like a lot of them, he had messaged me out of the blue one day saying he'd got my number from another guy I knew. The first couple of times we met, we just drove around in his car, drinking. It wasn't hard to see how he'd got his nickname – he was big, probably about twenty-five stone, and he looked to be somewhere in his forties. I thought he was OK at first. We talked. He told me about his wife and kids. We drove around and he bought me booze. Then, one day, when he came to pick me up, he had a takeaway kebab in a Styrofoam box on the front seat next to him. He offered me some but I wasn't hungry.

'Hey, I know,' he said. 'Let's go to my friend's place in Bradford. He's out today. We can sit down, I can eat this and we can relax properly. What do you think?'

I shrugged. *Why not?*

Big Maj drove us to the flat where he had his food and we shared a couple more drinks together. Then, without warning, he pushed me down onto the sofa. He was very forceful and, because of his size, I was afraid to say no. He fumbled at my jeans and, in a moment, he was on top of me. Fortunately it was over very quickly.

Afterwards I sat up and started doing up my clothes. Then, suddenly, I heard a key in the front door and another old guy walked into the flat – a complete stranger, about fifty years old, in baggy trousers and a T-shirt. He and Big Maj spoke in their own language then Big Maj turned to me. 'It's his flat. You have to pay him for using his flat.'

'What do you mean?' I said. 'I don't have any money. Anyway, I have to go now.'

I started to get up and walk towards the door and Maj got up too. He grabbed me and pinned me up against the wall.

'No!' he said angrily. 'You can't leave yet, Cassie. You have to pay him first.'

I looked at him, confused. Then the penny dropped. He didn't mean money. He meant I had to pay him in another way. I looked from Maj to the other guy – they were both big blokes, both older than me, and they were blocking my way. I didn't stand a chance. Maj let go of me then the older man took me into a tiny room with a single bed, locked the door and pinned me down with my hands above my head and raped me. He didn't say a word to me the whole time. Not one word. In that moment all my dignity disappeared. I wasn't a person any more, I was a *thing*. I was the 'money' to pay the guy.

As soon as he was finished, I fled. I grabbed my clothes and ran down the stairs and out of the door. Maj was there, standing by his car, casually smoking a cigarette, waiting for me. We drove back to Halifax in silence. He called and texted me for days afterwards but I ignored him. After a while the texts got really nasty and unpleasant but I just deleted them. I never wanted to see him again.

So what was Dad talking about, being a 'prostitute'? I never got anything from anybody. If anything, they took from me. Now Dad handed my phone over to Pete, 'for evidential purposes', and then told me I was grounded.

'You can only leave this house to go to school,' he said.

It didn't make a blind bit of difference. Blokes picked me up all hours of the day, even when I was walking to school. The next day I went out and got myself a new phone. Then, one morning in April, I awoke in a panic.

Where am I? I had no idea. I looked at the digital clock in the anonymous-looking hotel room and saw that it read 5:00 a.m. I shivered with cold and realised I was naked under a single thin sheet. Now I looked around me – there were no clues. The window looked onto a courtyard and the room was a mess. There were a couple of bags of drugs on top of the chest of drawers and I racked my brain to try and recall what had happened the night before. Slowly I picked up the two bags. It was coming back to me now – one was cocaine and the other was M-CAT. The M-CAT bag was still half full. Now I had flashbacks from the night before. I'd been picked up by a guy I'd never met before who, coincidentally, was also called Maj. We'd driven first to one guy's house and then another, where we'd got the drugs. Somehow we had ended up at this hotel and then three more men turned up. A burst of shame erupted in me as I remembered that one of the men had put his cock inside my mouth while another filmed it on his mobile phone. Then he pushed me back down on the bed and had sex with me while the other guy played with himself. Afterwards his friend climbed on top of me. The memories started to blur now. I had drunk a lot and taken a lot of drugs. And at some point I must have passed out.

Now I was alone and disorientated in a hotel room but I had no idea where the hotel was. I'd recently been taken to hotels in Huddersfield, Leeds and Manchester but I usually managed to get a lift home. I could be anywhere. Panic started to rise in my chest. Calm down, I told myself. Just try to stay calm. Shaking, I reached for my handbag and pulled out my mobile. I texted Pete: 'No credit. Please call.'

Just a few seconds later my phone rang. 'Cassie? Are you okay?'

Just the sound of his voice made me feel a little better. 'I don't know,' I replied, trying to cover the tremor in my voice. 'I don't know where I am.'

'Okay – well, look around you. Tell me what you can see.'

I looked around. 'I'm in a hotel room, but I don't know where.'

'Alright, stay calm, Cassie. Go downstairs to reception and ask them for the name and the address of the hotel. I'll come and get you as soon as I know where you are.'

The lady at the reception told me the name of the hotel I was at in Bradford and that's when I texted Pete.

'Stay where you are. I'm on my way,' he replied.

While I waited, I tried to tidy up the room and myself. The blokes had left their drugs and a tenner on top of the chest of drawers, presumably for my ride home. I grabbed them and put them in my bag. When Pete arrived with another officer, he told me I could get in the car while they checked the room. Then, on the way back to Halifax, Pete said they were taking me to the station for a debrief. There, they searched my bags.

'I'm afraid we're arresting you, Cassie,' said Pete.

'Why?'

'Because we found drugs in your handbag. We are arresting you for possession of a Class A drug.'

The police questioned me about what had happened the night before. I was vague myself on the details so I couldn't tell them much.

'Cassie,' Pete said firmly, folding his hands in front of him. 'Can I tell you what I saw in that hotel room? I saw condoms on the floor and blood on the bedsheets. That indicates there was a certain amount of sexual activity that went on. Did you have sex last night?'

I nodded.

'How many men?' asked Pete.

'I don't know. Three, I think.'

'Who were they?'

I shrugged. I honestly couldn't recall anybody's names except Maj's.

'Can you tell us anything more about these men?' Pete asked over and over again, but I didn't know anything about them myself.

'Did they know you are only fifteen?'

'I think so,' I replied. 'One of them did because he asked me my age.'

I didn't really understand why I'd been arrested; the drugs weren't mine and, as I kept telling them, I wasn't a prostitute. I never even bought the booze myself.

'They always offer me the alcohol,' I insisted. 'I've never even poured my own drinks. I suppose if I hadn't been drinking I probably wouldn't have agreed to the sex. It's not like I enjoy it. I drink lots so I don't feel the sex.'

'But, Cassie,' Pete sighed, exasperated, 'why do you get into the cars with them?'

I felt my eyes stinging with tears. 'I don't know,' I said quietly. 'I want someone to talk to, you know . . . have a drink with, have a smoke and chill out. It's just company, isn't it? It's not about the sex.'

In the end the police let me off with a final warning for possession, and Pete asked if he should drop me home. But after all that I couldn't face going back to my dad again, so Pete made some calls and a social worker turned up. I didn't recognise this one – I'd had so many over the years, and I never saw the same one twice. He told me that since they had nowhere else to put me I had to go into a children's home for a night, and that maybe the next day he would find alternative accommodation. He took me to the home, which was more like a hostel with lots of bedrooms and bathrooms, and I was shown to a small room on the second floor. Inside was a single bed, desk and a lamp, and curtains on the windows – that was it. There were lots of other children in the home – all of them younger than me – and they ran around making lots of noise all day long, but I just stayed in my room.

A couple of times an adult popped his head round my door to offer me food but I wasn't hungry. I just lay on my bed, hoping Social Services could find me somewhere else to stay as quickly as possible. Maybe I could stay with my sister or even my aunt? I couldn't bear the thought of seeing my dad again. Really, all I wanted was a smoke and a drink, and to get some rest. I was so tired.

Before I left the station that day, Pete had given me a meaningful look. 'You can't carry on like this, Cassie. You've got to let us help you.'

I smiled at him. I really didn't know what he meant.

9.

Akim

AKIM WAVED AT ME from his taxi across the street. I waved back. Then he did something unexpected: he held up a bottle of vodka and waved that at me. With his other hand he made a beckoning motion. I squinted at him for a second, not quite sure what he wanted. But then he waggled the bottle once more in the air and made the sign again to 'come here'. Amused, I went to speak to him.

'Hi, Akim,' I said, smiling. Akim was a local neighbour. Our houses were almost opposite each other. He was a family man – he worked all hours year-round as a taxi driver and then, in the summer, he also drove an ice cream van. I had known Akim and his wife Shazia all my life and had watched his two little boys growing up. They were probably the friendliest of all our neighbours, and every Christmas they came round with a box of chocolates for the family. They had known my mum too, and I think they had sympathy for me and my sisters, knowing we had grown up caring for her. Akim always gave me and my sisters free ice cream in the summer and, whenever we saw him, he'd greet me in a friendly way. Then, when I started high school, I would see him in his silver taxi as I got on the school bus.

'You're growing up too fast, Cassie!' he would shout jovially, and I'd smile.

Now I bent down to speak to him from where he sat in his taxi.

'Alright, Cassie? You want to go for a drink?' He held up the vodka bottle again.

Akim had never offered me alcohol before but he'd seen me drinking plenty of times in my back garden. In fact one afternoon he told me off when he spotted me with a can of lager.

'You're too young for alcohol nonsense,' he'd said in his broken English. I think he was originally from Pakistan.

'It's only a can,' I'd replied, shrugging. 'Besides, I like it. I've been drinking for years.'

'Far too young . . . too young . . .' Akim tutted and shook his head. Then he pointed towards the house. 'Mind your father doesn't see.'

'Oh, he doesn't care, Akim.'

'All fathers care. That is father's job.'

'Not mine,' I'd whispered under my breath. It was gutting to be living back with Dad again. After my arrest for possession of Class As, I'd stayed with Bernie again for a while, but that didn't last and after a couple of weeks I was sent back to Dad's place.

It came as a surprise to see him holding a large bottle of vodka. As far as I knew he was teetotal and a strict Muslim.

'Do you drink vodka, Akim?' I laughed. For some reason, the idea was quite strange. He seemed so straight to me.

'Oh, not often,' he said. 'Every now and then. Get in, we'll go for a drive and a drink.'

So I got in and Akim pulled out of our close and drove a few minutes up the road to an empty layby where we shared out the vodka. Then I rolled a joint and smoked that – Akim didn't want any. He said he had seen me getting into lots of cars recently and he even knew some of the people I'd been getting into the cars with.

'Oh yeah? Who's that, then?'

'My cousin Karim. You know Karim? Big tall man with a beard.'

'Erm . . .' I racked my brain. I knew so many guys who fitted that description and they only ever told me their nicknames, so I was never sure of their real names.

'Sure, you know him,' Akim persisted. 'You got in his car last Friday. He's got a silver Audi. Really nice car, fancy car. I saw you go off with him on Friday night.'

Now it was coming back to me. 'Oh, right.' I nodded. 'Yeah, I remember now. Karim was driving and he was with another guy I know. So that's your cousin, is it?'

'Yes, my cousin.'

Now Akim was silent for a moment and he looked down at the bottle of vodka in his lap. He seemed to be thinking about something, then he threw his head back and took a long, hard swig of the booze. Afterwards he handed the bottle to me and, as I took it, he looked me directly in the eye and said, 'I know what you did with Karim.'

I took the bottle from him but I didn't reply. I couldn't

remember myself what had happened that night. Like so many nights it was all a bit of blur. But the way he said those words: 'I know what you did', I knew he meant sex.

'I know what you do with all these guys, Cassie,' he went on, and there was something else behind those words, something menacing. 'They pick you up and then you go with them.'

I remained silent.

'Mmm?' he asked.

'I don't know, Akim,' I laughed, reaching out to touch the wooden worry beads hanging from the rear-view mirror. 'I'm usually wasted on a Friday night, so I don't really know. These beads are nice, where did you get them?'

I wanted to change the subject but he carried on. 'They give you something to drink and then you go with them, don't you? Some of them are strangers. You don't even know them. But you know me, don't you, Cassie?'

Now Akim slid his hand onto my knee and started moving it up and down my leg. I froze. *What was he doing? Akim was like a friendly uncle to me. He couldn't be trying it on, could he?*

'You know me and I know you very well. I know you . . .'

Disgusted, I picked up his hand and moved it off my leg. 'Yeah, I know you too, Akim,' I said crossly. 'And I know your lovely wife, Shazia. How is she, by the way? How's the baby?'

The couple had had another child in the last six months – a much longed-for baby girl. As far as I knew, they were devoted to one another and their three children. It wasn't right for him to act this way with me.

'Don't be like that, Cassie.' Akim put his hand back on my leg.

'You know we're friends, right?' Now he leant in very close and started to kiss my neck.

'You're a very pretty girl, Cassie,' he whispered. 'I've always liked you. We should be good friends, right?'

'No, no, this isn't right.' I squirmed as I felt his hot breath on my neck. I felt so uncomfortable with Akim making a move on me like this. He was a family friend. He'd known me since I was a child!

'Akim, what about your wife?' I implored. 'What about your children? Your new baby girl? You're a family man. A neighbour. Don't do this, please!'

I tried to get away but he had locked the taxi doors and now he had one arm wrapped tightly around me on my right side and the other was fumbling with my clothes. I kept squirming, trying to push him away from me, but he wouldn't let go.

'Cassie, don't say no to me,' he murmured, kissing my face. I tried to turn my head away but he forced his mouth onto mine. All the while he kept whispering: 'You don't say no to the other men and you don't know them. It's okay, it's just me, Akim. You know me. It's okay.'

He kept talking as he pulled down my leggings and then climbed on top of me. I struggled and kept saying 'No! No, Akim. Stop! Please!' but he wouldn't listen. I didn't want this. I *knew* him. I knew the faces of his children. But he overpowered me completely and I wasn't strong enough to get him off me. The only sound in the car now was Akim's grunts as he thrust himself inside me. I let the tears fall as I watched the worry beads swaying gently from the rocking motion of the car. Afterwards he sat back in his seat and I hastily pulled up my leggings. I was horrified. Of all the people who had forced themselves on me, this felt worse by a long way.

'Take me home,' I said in a flat voice.

'Sure,' he replied, and started the engine.

As we drove back to our close, my anger grew. This whole thing was planned just so he could take advantage of me, and all this time I had thought of him as a nice guy.

I've been such an idiot! I was taken in by him completely. The whole thing is just an act. Underneath the friendliness and jolly smile is just another arsehole. He's just like the rest. Well, he's not going to get away with it.

'I'm going to tell your wife,' I said through gritted teeth, my eyes focused on the road ahead. He stole a quick glance at me, and he must have known I was serious because I heard the panic in his voice now.

'Don't tell my wife,' he said quietly.

'I will. I'll tell Shazia what you did today, and I'll tell your boys too.'

There was a long silence, then Akim said slowly: 'I know your niece, Dara. Pretty girl. Pretty blue eyes, too, just like yours.'

What? Was he threatening my niece if I told his wife? I didn't say a word, so he carried on: 'I know where Dara lives. I've seen her lots of times. She's growing up fast, isn't she? Just like you.'

'Don't you dare go near her!' I exploded.

'I won't,' he replied calmly. 'And you won't tell my wife, will you?'

I sighed. 'No, I won't tell your wife.'

Akim dropped me at the end of our street, where I got out of his car and walked home. I could feel his eyes boring into me as I strode up the garden path and opened the front door. Then, with real anger, I slammed the door behind me. From that moment, every time I opened my front door I felt a knot of dread in my stomach at the thought of bumping into him again. Sometimes I would check up and down the street to make sure his taxi wasn't there before I left the house, because I knew that if he saw me, he might pull the same stunt. And now that I knew Dara was in his sights, I didn't have much choice but to protect her.

I saw his wife plenty of times after that incident, innocently walking her two boys to school, pushing the pram with their baby girl inside and chatting away to her children. He had betrayed her, just like he betrayed me, and I felt pity for her. She was being deceived by a man who posed as one thing but was actually something completely different. I hated him for what he had done. All I wanted to do was run up to her and tell her everything, describe exactly what her 'good husband' had done to me, but I couldn't. I couldn't say a word. Akim messaged me a couple of times after that, asking if I wanted to go out with him and chill, but I never replied to his messages. I couldn't bear to think about what had happened, let alone go out with him again. All I could do was try to avoid him altogether.

A couple of weeks later, a new youth offending team worker turned up at the house to discuss the offence for possession. She parked on the driveway in front of the kitchen window, and then came to the door.

'Liz Kearn.' She introduced herself to my dad with a brisk handshake and then said, 'I'd like to take Cassie out to McDonald's, if that's alright with you, Mr Pike?'

Dad didn't look at all happy about this. He usually liked all the meetings to take place in the house, so he could monitor what I was saying. 'Yeah, alright,' he reluctantly agreed.

I put my coat on and got into the passenger seat of Liz's car. Then she put the car into reverse, placing her arm over the back of my seat to get a better view out the back window, which meant she didn't see what happened next. As we slowly backed out of the driveway, Dad pulled back the net curtains in the kitchen and stood at the window, staring directly at me. He looked mean and mad and I felt a flutter of fear in my stomach. I knew what he was doing – it was a warning not to tell her anything. As usual, he'd given me a long list of 'things not to say' before her arrival and now he was making sure I had got the message. I nodded at him; I knew the drill by now. No discussion about his plants in the attic, or how he hit me, or his gambling or anything at all really. But he needn't have worried. Liz wasn't interested in him.

'So, Cassie, can you tell me how you got yourself into that situation in the hotel?' Liz asked me. I stirred my cup of tea in silence.

'Tell me, what do you remember about that night?' she tried again.

'I told the police everything I remember,' I sighed. I was sick of being questioned.

'I'm not the police, Cassie, I'm a member of the youth offending team and I'm here to try and help you stay out of trouble in the future. If we can work out how you came to be charged with possession of a Class A drug in the first place, perhaps we can stop it happening again.'

'The drugs weren't mine,' I sighed. 'I've said this before.'

'Yes,' she agreed. 'But we have to try and work out why you're the one with the drug offence. Did you know the men who gave you the drugs?'

'They're just friends,' I said, shrugging.

'How did you meet them?'

I took a long sip of my tea and stared out of the window. A blustery spring day had whipped up the branches of trees and the occasional dash of horizontal rain hit the window next to me. I traced the raindrop as it zigzagged down the pane. I wasn't going to give anything away. I didn't want to get anyone in trouble. It never even occurred to me to tell Liz about what happened with Akim. What would be the point?

Liz sighed, waiting for an answer, but I had no more to say. She asked several more questions but I only gave short, vague replies. After a while she sat back in frustration, folded her notes away and stared down at the table. She took a sip of her coffee and then looked out of the window. Together we sat in silence for a good few minutes until finally she said: 'You know, Cassie, after you turn sixteen we won't be able to help you any more. You'll not get this same level of protection from us, from the police or from any of the agencies currently working with you.'

I stared at her in disbelief. Protection! What protection? That was a joke. I looked after myself – that was something I'd been doing all my life.

'I don't care. I don't need any help,' I said defiantly. 'I'm going to move out when I'm sixteen and get my own place. In a few months' time, I can do what I want. I can leave home for good and never have to see my dad again. I can just be on my own and get away from all this rubbish. Then I won't have to keep coming to these meetings. Look, I've told you everything. Are we done here?'

'Yeah, I think so.' Liz shook her head. 'For now at least . . .'

10.

No Choice

'HEY SEXY. YOU CUMIN out 2nite?'

'Hi Caz, wanna chill?'

'I got sum coke and pills. You coming out?'

'Be outside at 6 p.m. Picking you up.'

'Hi Cassie – I'm Mo, Ali's mate. Wanna party 2nite?'

'Hey sexy, how are you? Do you want to come for a drink and smoke later?'

'Hey baby, are you free tonight? I have a bottle and a joint with your name on it.'

I scrolled through all the messages on my phone. Most of them I didn't bother replying to any more because I didn't know who they were from. It didn't seem to make much of a difference one way or another, because even if I told them I was busy or couldn't come out, they'd wait outside until I appeared and pick me up anyway. If I replied 'no', some got pissed off and would then call me from private numbers and leave messages calling me a 'white bitch' and a 'slag'. Sometimes it was hard to just get on with day-to-day life because the messages were so insistent. There were guys who just wouldn't give up, so even if I said 'no' three or four times they would still text me. There were times I said I couldn't come out and some guy might roll his car next to me as I walked down the street, hurling abuse at me, calling me a 'white slut' and threatening to harm me or my family. It was like being bombarded all the time. I didn't say anything to the social workers about this – what was the point? And anyway, I was scared of what the men might do if I told. They knew where I lived and they knew where my niece lived too. What would they do? I wondered. Hurt me? Kill me? It felt possible. After all, some of them were family men and they had a lot to lose.

I still tried to visit my sister Marie and spend time with Dara – these days it was the only thing that made me truly happy. I'd collect her from school and take her to the park, where she loved to go on the swings and roundabouts. Her delighted screams as I pushed her higher and higher on the swings made me so happy. With her, I felt like a child again; I could just be a kid and not worry about everything else going on in my world. But I was constantly looking over my shoulder, scared of being seen with her. I didn't want her to get dragged into my world. They could do what they liked to me but I couldn't bear to think of anyone going near Dara – she was still only nine years old.

One evening I was on my way home from visiting my sister when a silver car pulled up next to me with four Asian men in it. I didn't recognise any of them but I noticed that they were all laughing and seemed as if they were high on something. Two of them got out and started to mess around with me; one took my hand and twirled me around while the other one grabbed me from behind.

'Look at this gorgeous bum, fellas!' he laughed, as he put his hands all over me.

'Get off,' I said, trying to push his hands away, but he didn't stop. He didn't pay a blind bit of notice.

'She's got a nice arse,' the other one agreed, taking my arms and leading me into the car. I tried to squirm and get away but the man had a tight hold of me.

'Come on, darling, come for a ride with us,' he said, as he pushed me into the car and the guy inside made a grab for me so I couldn't escape. Then the first two guys got back in the car and they drove off.

I started to feel very panicky and scared. I had no idea who these guys were or where they were taking me. And I couldn't get away. There were two large men either side of me and both held me tightly. I was breathing hard, trying not to cry, but I didn't know what was going to happen. *Please don't kill me* was the only thought that went through my mind. *Please, please don't kill me*. The men seemed to know me but I didn't know any of them. At first I thought it was a joke, and that they would let me out again down the road. The way they were all laughing and talking in their language, I didn't know what was going on. But the car didn't stop – it drove on and I was firmly wedged inside. They passed round a joint but no one offered me any; it was like I didn't exist. They didn't talk to me at all, they just spoke to each other.

It was early evening and I saw that we were driving out of

town towards an industrial estate. Once there, we pulled off the main road, stopping in front of a warehouse. The guy in the front passenger seat got out and opened the large metal doors, then the car rolled forward into a dark warehouse. Suddenly it was pitch black and I couldn't see a thing. The men grappled me out of the car and put me on top of the bonnet. Then they all held me down, by my neck, hair, arms and legs, as one man climbed on top of me and started to have sex with me. I was too frightened to say no, too frightened to speak at all. I cried silently as they each took their turn while the others held me down.

I tried not to think about what was happening. It was cold and the only light came from the headlamps on the car, which threw long black shadows of the men against the walls. Who were they? Why did they pick me up? It felt like they knew who I was, but how? I just wanted it all to be over but I had no idea what they might do next. Once they were done, they let me go and I pulled my clothes back on. Then they nodded towards the car and I got back in. Now I pleaded for my safe return.

'Please, I just want to go home now. Please just let me go.' And to my relief, they agreed.

'Alright, alright, don't make a bloody song and dance about it,' the driver shouted to me. 'I'm taking you back. Now shut up and stop fucking whining!'

To my great relief, I saw that we were retracing the journey that had taken us out of town, and as we turned the corner towards the road they had picked me up from, I felt a desperate desire to jump out. Finally the car stopped and they let me out. Then they drove off. I stood rooted to the spot as I watched the car disappear down the road and, for a moment, I dared not move. I felt my chest rising and falling as I panted heavily. But then, once I saw they had gone completely, I dissolved into tears. The way they had treated me, it was like I was nothing. Worse than nothing. I felt so low, so worthless. All I wanted was to get home and have a smoke. I practically ran the rest of the way home, shaking all the way. In my head I could hear the echoes of their laughter in the large, cavernous warehouse, taunting, tormenting me. I had to block the memory from my mind; I had to obliterate it from my head altogether.

On my way home I passed the corner shop where I bought my booze and fags.

'Hey, Mango,' I said. Mango was a new shopkeeper – he had taken over from the previous owner a few months earlier, and when I asked him his name he had given me a difficult-sounding reply. I tried to pronounce his name but didn't succeed, and he had laughed and said not to worry, I could call him 'Mango, like the fruit'. He was friendly, probably in his mid-thirties, a short man with brown hair and eyes.

'Cassie.' He nodded from behind the counter.

I counted the coins in my purse – not enough to get a drink. 'Can I get a bottle of vodka? I'll give you the money tomorrow.'

'Yeah sure.'

He gave me the bottle and I unscrewed the cap as I walked out, taking small swigs all the way home. I knew I had a few pills under my bed, so I could take those too. And then, well, everything would be okay. As long as I could forget, it would all be okay.

I lived in the moment. I lived to get high. In the morning I was usually still wasted from the night before, and that's how I liked it. Even when I woke up completely wrecked I still took something to stop me coming down later on. I just couldn't face it. Being straight meant dealing with reality, and that was something I couldn't cope with. Some days I woke up in my own bed, some days I woke up in a hotel room, and other days I woke up on a bare mattress in a house I didn't recognise with a stranger sleeping next to me. I'd creep out the front door, hoping for a clue as to how to get home. There were nights I'd be picked up and taken to a pub or a restaurant, where there were always plenty of drugs going around – coke, M-CAT, fet, pills. I took it all, and after a while everything would become hazy and then I'd pass out. I'd come round in the early hours of the morning, my head banging against a hard, concrete floor, wondering what the hell was happening. A few seconds later, I'd focus enough to see I was on the floor of the toilets during a lock-in, being fucked by some stranger, completely naked. Oh God, I'd think to myself, recoiling at the smell of urine next to my head. *I need to take something because it really isn't worth returning to the real world for this!* They didn't talk to me much, these men. They didn't ask me if I was okay or how I was doing. Usually they only communicated with me to offer me more drugs. I came to expect that they would only talk to each other, and in a language I didn't understand.

Then there was the day I woke up in a house covered in bare mattresses, with several men asleep nearby. *What is this place? Who are these people?* I wondered, as I tried to pick my way through the unconscious figures without stepping on an arm or a leg. No beds, no headboards, covers or sheets, just a load of mattresses. It was weird, but I didn't dwell on it. All I wanted was to find my way home. Anyway, it was just one of the many weird places I had woken up in over the past few months. I didn't seem to have a handle on it any more. I had no control. These days, I was taken all over the place – to Leeds, Manchester, Huddersfield, Bradford – and I'd be gone for days at a time, coming round three days later in a car to be dropped back at the place from where I'd been picked up.

The only person I trusted was Pete. He was always there for me. If I felt threatened or couldn't get home, I'd call him and ask him to come and get me, and no matter where I was or what time of day it was, he'd come. And though he didn't judge me or tell me off, he did talk to me about my future.

'This path you're going down, Cassie, it's not a good one,' he sighed one day, as he drove me back from a hotel where he'd found me in the early hours. 'It doesn't end well. Trust me, I've seen it. Cassie, these guys are dangerous. These situations you're getting into, they're dangerous. You think these guys are your friends but they're not. The problem is that I can't help you like this, just picking you up all the time from these places. The only way I can help you is to get you out of harm's way altogether.'

'What do you mean?'

'I mean, get you away from these men. Get you to a place where they can't find you any more.'

I thought about this for a second. My phoned beeped with the arrival of another text message. 'Out of harm's way' sounded good. 'How?'

'You have to agree to go into care. That's the only way we can protect you properly.'

I thought about this for a while – it was true, I didn't want them calling me all the time, texting me, picking me up off the streets. I felt trapped and out of control but, at the same time, I didn't trust the authorities. It was like my dad said: 'Give 'em an inch and they'll take a mile.' I didn't want to be controlled by Social Services either.

'No thanks,' I told him firmly. 'I'm fine.'

'You're not fine, Cassie. You're really not fine, and if you continue down this path, making these choices, then I really fear for your safety. Think about it. Please.'

I liked Pete, I trusted him and I truly believed that he was trying to help me. I just had no confidence that the police or Social Services could do anything to make my life better. After all, they had been around for years now and what good had that done me?

One warm evening in May, I was on my way home from meeting Simone when I went into the corner shop for some fags. It feels like summer already, I thought dreamily to myself, as I felt myself drifting upwards from the M-CAT I'd taken earlier. On top of that I'd smoked a couple of joints, so I was feeling good, really spaced out.

'Hey, Mango,' I said. 'Can I get twenty Richmond?'

'Sure, Cassie – you want drink tonight?'

'Hmmm?'

'I have drink in back of shop. Just closing now. Come and have drink with me.'

Mango pulled aside the beaded curtain behind him that separated the shop from the rest of the house. I walked through and saw that there were two bedrooms along the corridor and a small living room at the back. I looked in – there wasn't much in the way of furniture: a mattress to sit on, a small table and stacks of brown boxes.

'Just one minute,' Mango called out to me, as he returned to the front of the shop, turned out the lights, flipped over the sign to 'Closed' and bolted the door. There was a small bottle of vodka and some Coke cans on the coffee table. I helped myself to a drink and felt happy as the fiery liquid slid down my throat. Anything not to have to go home! I'd had another row with Dad recently and this time Rose said she'd had enough and that they couldn't cope with my behaviour. She said they didn't want me at home any more. Well, that was fine by me – I didn't like living with them either. The only problem was I didn't have anywhere else to go.

'You like?' Mango offered me a cigarette and I took it. I thought it must be wonderful to run a corner shop and have all the booze and fags you want at any time. And chocolate! He had tons of chocolate. I looked closely at the boxes and read some of the labels: *Drifters, Mars, Yorkie, Dairy Milk, Twirl*. Mmmm . . . that sounded nice. My head swam pleasantly and I took a long, slow pull on the fag.

'Hey, this isn't bad, is it?' I laughed.

'No, not bad,' said Mango, crossing his legs next to me. He was wearing his usual clothes – a jumper, jogging bottoms and sandals. 'Just work too much. Too many hours working. Not enough relax for Mango.'

'What are the rooms for?' I asked, indicating the bedrooms along the corridor.

'Is for rent. Owner rents them for money.' He made the motion for money by rubbing his thumb and forefinger together.

'Oh, so you're not the owner?' I asked, surprised.

'No, no, no, just work here. That's all.'

We drank for about an hour and I was getting really relaxed, so I closed my eyes. The next thing I knew Mango was climbing on top of me, pushing me back onto the mattress and wriggling out of his trousers.

'Mango! What are you doing?' I pushed him off.

'Cassie – you have drink and now we have sex, yes?'

'NO! I don't want to have sex with you.'

'Please, I give you the drink.' He gestured towards the mostly empty bottle of vodka.

'So? Just because you give me some drink, doesn't mean I have to have sex with you.'

'Yes, yes. This is what you owe me now.'

Then he came towards me and pushed me back down on the mattress again. I tried to struggle to get out from under him but he just carried on, taking off my jeans and holding down my arms. Then he put himself inside me and I was too out of it to stop him. At some point I heard a door open and I looked past him to see that another man had emerged from one of the bedrooms. He looked really old, in his fifties, and he was very fat. He wore jeans and a large, stained T-shirt that stretched over his belly. The man walked down the long corridor towards us and then, as soon as

Mango had finished, he unbuttoned his trousers and climbed on top of me without saying a word.

Oh Jesus. I closed my eyes and tried to imagine this wasn't happening. The man was so fat and he smelt horrible. I hated every moment. As soon as he'd finished I got up and put my clothes back on and returned to the front of the shop. On my way I passed an open cardboard box full of cigarette cartons. I reached in and pulled out two large cartons, each containing forty boxes of cigarettes, and put them into my large, over-the-shoulder bag. Then I walked out and never went back there again.

I staggered down the street, half laughing, half crying. *Ha, that'll show him. That's what he owes me!* I stumbled and fell but then I picked myself up again. *Fucking Mango! He won't try that again.*

11.

Giving Up

I COULD RUN AWAY. I could just get on a bus and leave Halifax for good. But where would I go? I don't have any money and, besides, I don't know anybody. How would I earn money? Where would I sleep? How would I survive?

The same questions went round and round in my head as I lay in bed, squinting against the bright June sunlight that streamed through my curtains. I looked at the clock. It was just past midday and this was another day that I hadn't made it into school. According to my teachers, my attendance was at an all-time low of fifty-nine per cent, and though I was meant to be taking two GCSEs that month, I hadn't done any of the work so I knew they would be a disaster. It hardly seemed worth turning up any more. I was only going in to stop Dad getting fined so he didn't get mad at me. But honestly, what was the point? What was the point of anything any more? I closed my eyes and curled up into a tight ball as I felt the crushing weight of dread on my chest.

Nothing feels good any more. I don't even want to step outside the

*house because I know what's waiting for me out there – more of the
same. This is no life, no life at all.*

The past few days had been a blur. It had all started out okay
. . . I'd met up with a guy I knew called Goldie – everyone called
him that because he had one bright gold tooth at the front of
his mouth. Goldie was Asian, in his late twenties and a dealer.
After he picked me up we rode around in his car for a while,
delivering weed and pills. Quite late we ended up in a layby
and there, another car pulled up with two guys I didn't know.
Goldie got out and started chatting to these other guys. Then
he opened the car door and said I should get in their car and go
with them.

'I don't want to,' I replied. 'I don't know them.'

'It's okay, Cassie, don't worry,' he reassured me, beckoning me
with his hand. 'Nothing bad is gonna happen. You go with them
now and I'll meet you later on. Okay?'

I shook my head again, no.

'Look, I've got a few pills here for you and a bag of weed. You
take this and go with them.'

He handed me the drugs but I still didn't want to go with the
men. By now I knew exactly what would happen if I went with
them. I knew they would all want sex from me.

'But I don't know them, Goldie,' I objected.

'Don't be silly, Cassie.' Goldie opened the door and took me
firmly by the arm, then guided me to the other car. 'It's all fine.
Just get in and I'll see you later. Okay?'

The door opened and I found myself in the back of a stranger's
vehicle. Then the door clicked shut behind me and I heard the

locks going down. I took out the little bag of pills Goldie had given me and swallowed one.

'I'll see you later,' Goldie called, as the car engine started and we pulled away. Of course I didn't see him again that night.

'Where are we going?' I asked the man in back seat next to me.

'We're going to a house party in London,' he said, smiling. 'It's gonna be great. You'll have a great time.'

Really? We're going to a house party? I was pleased – this sounded good, although London was a long way from Halifax. It turned out to be a long journey, so I took more of the pills and drank whatever came my way. At some point I came round to find that I was lying on a mattress and some guy I didn't know was having sex with me. What kind of house party is this? I wondered in a daze, before I took another couple of pills. There were no other girls there, just me and all these Asian men. The curtains were actually bedsheets strung across the windows and the rooms were filled with bare mattresses, nothing more. It felt like some kind of drugs den. At one point I came round to see a bloke standing over me, counting out some notes, but then I blacked out again. It all seemed to happen to someone else in another world, another time. I came round again and I was back in the car.

'What day is it?' I asked wearily, as I rubbed my face.

'Wednesday.'

'Wednesday?' I had lost three whole days and I had no idea where I'd been or what had happened to me. Some house party that was!

Now I slowly inched out of my bed and grabbed at my handbag. I pulled out my phone – the inbox had seventeen new messages in it. I didn't want to look at any of them. Instead I rooted around to see what drugs I had left. Half a packet of fags, about a third of a bottle of vodka, the remnants of bag of the weed and . . . *what's this?* Incredibly my hand landed on a small plastic bag containing half a dozen pills. For a moment my mood lifted as I realised I had enough drugs to get me through the next couple of days. Get me through to what, though? The thought came crashing into my mind: *Get me through . . . why? Why bother? It's just more of the fucking same.* My fingers closed around the small bag and I knew what I was going to do with those pills. I heaved myself out of bed and pulled on my jeans and a sweatshirt. I slipped on my trainers, pulled my handbag over my shoulder and tiptoed to the toilet. If there was anyone in the house I really didn't want to bump into them today. After locking the door, I opened the bathroom cabinet and shoved aside the shampoo bottles and calamine lotion to see what was lurking behind. *Aha* – I was in luck: some paracetamol and a few capsules of Nurofen. I counted them out – nine altogether. That was probably enough. I stuck the pills in my handbag and crept out of the house.

Outside it was a beautiful June day – bright-pink blossom covered the trees and the air felt fresh and warm at the same time. I headed for the large oak tree in the park where I liked to hang out on my own. It was quiet and peaceful there, just what I needed. It's better this way, I thought to myself, as I walked, head down, trying not to catch anyone's eyes.

Who would care if I disappeared tomorrow? Not Dad, that's for sure. He doesn't want me in the house any more and I don't want to be around him either. I'm nothing but a punchbag to him. Maybe my sisters might be sad for a while but they'll get over it. My niece will miss me, it's true, but this is better for her. This way she doesn't get dragged into my ugly, sordid world.

I thought of her happy, smiling face and tears sprung to my eyes. I loved her so much, and I didn't want to leave her, but this was for the best.

My life wasn't worth living any more, and I didn't want to wake up feeling this way any more. I didn't want to wake up at all. The only feelings I had left now were fear . . . and dread. Dread of what might happen the next day, dread of remembering what had happened to me the night before, dread of being sober, dread of being picked up, dread of remembering the termination. I was constantly on the run from myself – frightened that one day it would all catch up with me. I couldn't take living in this state of constant fear. I was tired of the running. I wanted out.

I sat down on the grass, leant up against the large trunk of the oak and got out my fags. Knowing what I was about to do I felt nervous and my hands shook a little with fear. Would it hurt? I hoped not. I hoped I could just fall asleep and never wake up again. I lit a cigarette and took a long, hard draw – that at least helped to stop the thumping of my heart against my chest. Now I laid the pills out before me – fifteen in total. It was enough, I knew, to send me somewhere else. I slowly unscrewed the cap off the vodka and, one by one, I downed the pills. First, Goldie's pills – what were they? I didn't even know. Curious, I examined one to see what it had on it. They often had little symbols to identify them – Mitsubishis, Mercedes, Dolphins or something else. The symbol looked like a little shell. I didn't know what that meant and, frankly, I didn't care. I just swallowed it down with all the others. Soon they were gone, so I started on the paracetamol. Only five of these, each 200mg, and finally the Nurofen. Four. That should be plenty, I thought to myself, as I swallowed the last one. I lit a joint and smoked it all the way down to the roach, listening to the sounds of the town around me: laughing groups of kids hanging out by the fountain, car horns blaring, police sirens wailing somewhere in the distance, the continual thrum of traffic. Soon it would all be gone.

I lay down and waited for death to take me.

Now. I want to go now. That way I won't feel any pain any more. I won't be used and abused. I won't be frightened all the time, ashamed all the time, sad all the time.

The tree above me buckled and bent in the wind. Something shifted and I felt myself drifting upwards through the leaves. The breeze caught me as I floated up, up, up towards the sky. I left my body and became part of the sky, expanding and changing, like the clouds around me.

I am drifting away . . . drifting on a sea of clouds, changing shape every second. Oh my God, it's her! I see my mother's face. She's smiling at me. She looks the way she did many years earlier, when she was well enough to speak, well enough to hold me. She reaches out towards me and her arms embrace me in a warm, protective cuddle. I feel a swell of happiness inside. It's so good to be in her arms again. To feel her warmth and love wrap around me. 'I am with you,' she whispers. 'I am here. Don't be afraid.' I let myself rest in her arms and everything goes dark.

Drip. Drip. Drip.

Something wet lands on my nose. I swat it away. Another drip plops on my cheek. My hand moves towards my face but it feels weirdly detached from my body. Is this my hand? It feels like it belongs to someone else. I push away the moistness on my cheek but I can't feel my face. I take in a sharp breath and realise I'm cold and shivering. My eyes open to see the rain falling gently from the tree above. Plop, plop – each raindrop explodes around my head like a wet grenade. How long have I been here? My stomach turns over – I feel sick. And then it hits me: oh no, it didn't work. I'm still alive! But now I'm cold and soaked through under this tree. And I haven't got a clue what time it is. Or even what day it is. I want to sit up but my body tells me this is not a good idea. As soon as I lift my head up the world swims and expands around me. I'm high as kite. Maybe higher. My mouth is dry and my tongue thick and swollen. I try to swallow but it's hard. I'm so dizzy and disorientated I can't seem to make anything stay in one place but I know I can't stay here any longer. I have to get home and dry.

Very, very slowly I sat up and I let the world carry on spinning until it was still enough for me to move again. Then, gingerly, I pushed myself up to my feet, sensing the strange aches in my joints from lying on the hard ground for so long. It was nearly night-time and the park was bathed in a gentle orange glow from the setting sun. It looked like a beautiful evening. Around me I saw couples strolling hand in hand, young mums pushing prams and boisterous teenagers kicking footballs. I had never felt lonelier in my whole life.

I sighed and walked home.

12.

Anger Rising

IF YOU WERE TO ask me today, 'What happened?', I could tell you, but I couldn't back then. I didn't know what was going on. I thought I was so grown up, so smart, but the truth was I didn't understand anything until after it was all over. I thought I was just unlucky, meeting so many guys who wanted to have sex with me. I thought that if it wasn't my bad luck then maybe this was the norm, this was how guys always behaved towards women. I never saw the pattern. I never connected the pieces of the puzzle. The drugs didn't help – most of the time I was in such a fug I could barely think about getting through the day, let alone sit down to consider what was going wrong in my life. I just thought that I was getting into bad situations of my own making – it never occurred to me for a minute that these encounters were anything other than accidental. I felt hurt and angry at what was happening but I didn't know what I could do to stop it and I blamed myself for getting into the mess to start with. I woke up every day with fresh bruises on my knees, arms and wrists, love bites all over my neck, legs and arms and no memory of how they got there. Summer had begun but I couldn't wear a short-sleeved dress or a knee-high skirt because my body was black and blue. And, just as I didn't make a connection between the encounters, I didn't see that the bruises were getting worse, the trips out of Halifax more frequent, or the incidents more brutal.

One warm night in early June a car stopped with two guys in it – it was Maj and Maj's cousin Bilal from our night in the hotel. Maj was driving.

'Come on, Caz,' Maj beckoned me from inside the car. 'We've got something to drink and a little bit to smoke. Why don't you come for a drink and a chill with us?'

Bilal got out and opened the passenger door for me. 'Come on, Caz. Hop in.'

It was like an invitation, but not one I felt I could turn down. So I got into the front seat of the car and we drove off.

'Where are we going?' I asked, as we headed out of town and towards the motorway.

'Manchester, darling!' shouted Bilal from behind me, above the roar of the traffic.

'Where's your friend tonight?' I asked Maj, recalling the third guy who had been with us at the hotel in Bradford.

'Oh, he's got to work,' Maj said.

'Yeah, he's working. Shame, really,' Bilal said, and the pair of them laughed.

I leant onto the car door and let the breeze blow my hair around as we sped up the M62. For a brief second I closed my eyes and tried not to think about the exam I was meant to be taking at school the next day. It was my first English GCSE and I had hardly looked at the books at all. The school had been really good to me of late and had adjusted my schedule so that I would sit just two GCSEs this year. Even so, the work was more than I could manage. I should have been revising tonight – staying at home, getting a good night's sleep, resting, all the things the teachers had told us were sensible ways to prepare for an exam. Getting into this car for a smoke and a chill probably wasn't the best idea, but then, well, what choice did I have? And it wasn't like I was expecting to do well anyway.

Bilal passed me a joint from the back seat and I took a long drag. At least a joint would be a nice way to relax before an exam. It was a pleasant drive to Manchester and I enjoyed the feeling of getting away from it all.

We pulled into a large empty car park in an industrial estate just as the sun was dipping low in the sky. Maj turned off the engine, yawned and stretched his arms out in front of him.

'Oh God, I need a drink!' he said.

Bilal passed him the bottle of vodka and he poured a large measure into a plastic cup and topped it up with Coca-Cola, then he poured another cup for me. He turned up the music and rolled a joint. Meanwhile, in the backseat, Bilal got out a little wrap of coke and started cutting it up with his credit card on the back of a CD case. We sat and drank and then, after a little while, we each snorted a fat line. The white powder shot up my nose and exploded into my sinuses. *Urgh.* I always hated the first line of coke – it tasted so bad, like chemicals, and made me want to gag. So I took a big swig of my drink to chase the taste away.

Before long, though, my throat and gums were numb and my head buzzed pleasantly. I felt quite peaceful, serene even. The guys were talking among themselves as Bilal rolled another joint, so I smoked a cigarette out the window, puffing large billowy clouds out of the car.

Mmmm . . . this was definitely a nice way to relax before my exam. No stress here.

'I need to get out,' I told the two men after a while. 'I need a wee.'

'Sure.' Maj nodded towards the dark end of the car park. 'Look, there's a big tree over there and there's no one around. You might as well use that.'

Good idea, I thought woozily to myself, as I got out of the car and rose unsteadily to my feet. Closing the door behind me, the sound of the car stereo was now small and muffled and I suddenly noticed the silence and emptiness of the car park. There really was nobody around here. The place was dark and very still. Trying to stay upright, I headed towards the large tree on the far side of the car park and, as I walked, I became aware of the sound of my shoes on the asphalt. *Click clack, click clack* went my heels – a little sound that was engulfed by the giant silence of the place. I tried to be as quick as possible, squatting down behind the tree, looking around furtively to double check there were no strange men lurking in dark corners. As quick as I could, I pulled my clothes back up and teetered back to the car. I shivered now from the cool night air. I wanted to get back in the car where it was warm. Opening the car door, the thumping techno beats came blaring out.

'There you are!' Maj greeted me as I got back in. 'Look what I've got for you.' He handed me the large plastic tumbler filled with vodka and Coke.

'Oh, thanks,' I said, taking the drink. Time seemed to slip by so quickly now, I lost track of how long we had been in the car park. At some point I tried to light a fag but I dropped my lighter in the footwell and it was dark down there, so I had to root around with my hand to try to find it. But instead of my lighter, my hand landed on something cold, long and smooth. It felt like a wooden handle. Curious, I tried to lift it up but it was very heavy on one side. I put my other hand down and brought it up towards the light in the centre of the car. It was a hammer.

'Why have you got a hammer in here?' I asked the men, showing Maj and Bilal the tool. In an instant, Bilal took the hammer from me, shifted himself behind my seat and then quickly brought the hammer round my left side and underneath my neck, pinning me back in my seat. Then Maj leaned over and started to kiss me and pull my top down. I couldn't move. I could barely swallow. I wanted to say, 'Get off', but my voice came out small and strangulated.

The hammer under my neck kept me fastened back in the seat while Maj climbed on top of me and raped me. Helpless, I lay there as he did what he wanted and then climbed off me. Bilal was in the back playing with himself, so he no longer held the hammer round my neck. As soon as I saw my chance, I opened the car door and threw myself out.

Ooof! I landed face first on the hard ground but I quickly picked myself up and tried to dress myself. Maj was buttoning his shirt up, a stupid grin on his face, and in that second I felt a surge of anger.

The bastard! I'm so sick of this shit. I'm so tired of being helpless all the time, fucked over all the time, and that bastard held a hammer to my neck! How dare he!

Furious, I grabbed the hammer and brought it down hard on Maj's knee. He cried out in pain and I swung again, this time towards Bilal.

'Fucking hell!' Bilal shouted, as he swerved to avoid the hammer and, because I missed, I lost my balance and toppled over. At that moment, Maj, yelling in pain, slammed the passenger door shut and started the engine. I was still sprawled on the ground as he put the car into reverse and I watched with a sort of deranged satisfaction as they drove out of the car park. Slowly, I rose to my feet.

'Yeah, you better run, you fuckers! I'll smash you up!' I shouted after them, brandishing the hammer, laughing at their cowardice.

'Not such tough guys now, are you?' I shouted again into the darkness, and it was then I noticed my mouth felt odd. I put my hand to my face and felt around. Half my front tooth was missing.

Oh well. At least those bastards are gone.

I dropped the hammer and suddenly all the energy left my body. It was dark, late and I was alone in a car park in Manchester. How the hell was I meant to get home?

Drunk and disorientated, I staggered towards the exit of the car park and tried hard to think which way we had come in. This was a big, busy road, so I guessed it would probably take me back home eventually. I calculated that if I started to walk now I might be home by the morning. Then again, I might not. There was really nothing else I could do, so I started to walk in the direction I figured was Halifax.

I walked and I walked and I walked, and I tried not to think about the hammer attack in the car. It made me so angry to think about what they did. Had they been planning it all along? Why? Why attack me like that? Did it give them some kind of a kick? At least I'd fought back this time and didn't let the fuckers get away with it. I was so tired . . . so tired of this shit. I just wanted to get home and rest. God, I needed some rest.

I noticed there were tears coursing down my cheeks but I just kept walking.

I walked and walked and at some point the sun came up. I was half asleep, half awake, my mind far away in another place when the car slowed down and pulled up on the kerb in front of me. To my relief I saw there was a bright-yellow TAXI sign on top of the car. I walked towards the car and bent down to see a concerned-looking face staring back at me.

'Are you alright, love?' the man asked. He was in his forties, this Asian man, and he seemed so genuine I nearly cried.

'No, I've got to go home . . . going to Halifax,' I slurred, and told him my address.

'Oh right.' The man frowned. 'I've just finished my shift but, well, you look like you need a lift. Your lip is swollen, by the way, and I think it's been bleeding. Did you know that?'

I put my hand to my mouth. 'I chipped a tooth too,' I explained.

'Halifax is a long way. It's going to cost a few quid. Have you got money?'

'Yeah, I've got money at home. I can pay you when we get there. Can you take me?'

He sighed. 'Yeah, alright. Get in. You're not going to be sick, are you? If you feel sick at any point, you must tell me and I'll stop the car. I can't have you making a mess of my seats.'

'No, it's alright. I'm not going to be sick.'

With relief, I opened the car door and fell into the back seat. It was a good hour back to Halifax so I closed my eyes for a brief second and went to sleep.

'We're here, love,' the taxi driver announced. *What? Already?* It felt like I had barely shut my eyes. Now I caught sight of the digital clock on the dashboard. 8:10 a.m., it read.

'Is that really the time?' I gasped. 'Ten past eight?'

'Yup,' the driver confirmed. Where had the night gone? Panic fluttered in my chest as I remembered I had to sit an exam today. I had to be in school for 8.30!

'Okay, look, my money's in the house,' I said. 'Can you just wait for me, please, while I go in and get changed and then drop me at school afterwards. I'll pay you. Just stay there, please.'

'Yeah, alright,' he sighed again. 'Just be quick, yeah? I should have been home an hour ago.'

I dashed inside the house and went straight upstairs to change into my school uniform. I also got out fifty pounds I'd stashed under my bed. Then I went to the bathroom, splashed some water on my face and took a brief look in the mirror. *Oh shit, my face was a mess.* My lip was bruised and swollen and my front tooth was chipped. There was also a fair amount of grazing on my chin and face. I wiped the dried blood from my face, combed my hair and put on a fresh face of make-up. Then I headed quickly to the front door, keen to avoid a confrontation with Dad or Rose. I got back in the cab and we drove the ten minutes to my school.

I felt very odd as we approached the school in the taxi and I saw the other kids swarming in through the school gates, chatting to each other in pairs and groups, just like any other day. I bet no one had had a night like mine! My heart sank at the thought of having to go in there and pretend that everything was normal, but I knew I had to do it.

'Thanks,' I said, shoving the money into the taxi driver's hands. He counted it quickly and then looked at me sceptically.

'You're taking an exam today?' he asked.

I nodded.

'Good luck, love,' he said, before driving off. I stood outside the gates for a second, my heart thumping at the effort of getting myself ready for school when I was still drunk and out of it from the night before. Then I felt around in my handbag for a fag. I couldn't do this without a cigarette first. Shakily, I brought the long white cylinder to my lips and lit it, taking a long slow drag. I tried to keep my eyes down; I didn't want to talk to anybody today. I'll just go in and do it, I told myself. No harm in giving it a go. I took another pull of the cigarette and blew smoke out in front of me. Then I perched up against the brick wall as I tried to compose myself.

Brrrring! Brrrring! Brrrring!

The school bell sounded and the last of the students made their way inside. Was I going in? I still wasn't sure.

One of the teachers approached me as the playground emptied. 'Are you alright, Cassie?'

I just stared at her.

'Your lip looks swollen. What's happened?'

'I was out last night. I was in a car with some guys and they took me to Manchester and then, well, they attacked me in the car, so I jumped out but I landed on my face and then I hit one of them with a hammer . . .'

The teacher drew a sharp breath in. 'You've got a nasty split lip, Cassie.'

'Yeah, and a broken tooth and all. I just don't know if I should go into the exam this morning.'

The teacher looked at me hard, biting her lip. 'Have you slept?'

'Erm, not really.'

'Well, you're here,' the teacher sighed. 'You could give it a go, I suppose. And then we'll see if we can't help you get that tooth and lip seen to. Do you think you're up for giving it a go?'

I shrugged, put out the fag and jumped off the wall.

The rest of the day was a blur. I don't remember taking the exam. I don't know if I even made much of an attempt at the questions. As soon as I sat down and the invigilator told us to turn over our exam papers, a wave of tiredness swept over me. I must have stuck it out for a while but I don't remember what I wrote. The next thing I knew I was at the hospital but I don't remember how I got there or what happened to me when I was there. At some point Pete turned up and I told him everything I could remember from the night before. He took notes in his little notepad, just as he had so many times before, and he asked what I wanted to do.

Tears sprang to my eyes. 'I want out,' I whispered. 'I've had enough. I'm sick of it.'

Pete nodded. 'You know what this means, Cassie. This means we'll put you in police protection and then place you in foster care. You won't be going back to your family home. Is that what you want?'

I nodded. I couldn't fight it any more. I couldn't fight them. I had to get away. 'I just want it to stop.'

13.

No Change

PETE AND JUNE STOOD either side of me at the door of the small terraced house in Sowerby Bridge. It had been a short journey from the police station in Halifax – just twenty minutes – but to me it felt like a massive step. *I was going to live with a foster family! A new family.* It was a bizarre thought. After all, I already had my own family, so it was strange to think I was going to be living with a different family: people I didn't know, people who had never met me before. It had taken June a few hours to secure a placement but she seemed pleased to tell me in the late afternoon that she had found a lovely couple who were happy to take me in.

I didn't really want to leave Halifax and my family behind but I was so desperate to escape my situation and living with Dad just wasn't an option any more. He didn't want me anywhere near him or Rose. He had made that perfectly clear. But I had just been raped with a hammer held to my neck – what would be next? I had to get away, and this was my only chance. Still, it was hard to walk away from everything I knew into a completely unknown household. I shook, but I didn't know if it was from nerves or from the lack of drugs. *Damn, I could do with a smoke right now.*

An old man with a mop of white hair came to the door wearing a dark-green jumper and beige trousers.

'Yes, hello,' he said croakily. 'Come in. Follow me.'

We all followed him down the small corridor to the kitchen at the back of the house where a woman, his wife, I assumed, was standing by the cooker. This was my new foster family? They both looked so old. More like foster grandparents than foster parents!

Pete led the introductions: 'Cassie, this is Mr and Mrs Carrington, Mark and Sarah. Mark, Sarah – this is Cassie.'

'Hullo,' I said meekly.

'Nice to meet you, Cassie,' the older lady said politely. 'We're very pleased to have you here. I hope you'll be very comfortable in our home. Would you like a cup of tea or would you like to see your room first?'

'I don't know. I don't mind,' I replied. I felt shy in front of these strangers and confused by the formality of the situation. Meanwhile my phone buzzed in my handbag.

'What about her bags?' Mark asked June. 'Shall I help you get them from the car?'

'She doesn't have much at the moment.' June said, nodding at the one suitcase of belongings I had managed to retrieve from Dad's house. 'But we'll go to her family home and bring back anything else she might need in the next few days.'

Pete and June stayed just ten minutes longer, then left. I felt odd and out of place in this neat and quiet house. It seemed very nice but Mark and Sarah explained that they had retired and their children had grown up and left home some years earlier, so now it was just them in the house. They showed me upstairs to a tidy little bedroom overlooking the street. The bedding and most of the furniture was cream and there were pictures of flowers on the walls. I unpacked my make-up and hair straighteners and the few clothes I had, then wandered downstairs and through the kitchen door, out into the garden. Trying to calm my nerves, I lit a cigarette. As I puffed away, I checked the messages on my phone.

'Where r u? Tell me now!'

'Comin out tonight? Have a bottle I owe u.'

'Coming over to see you tonight. Be ready.'

'U better tell me where u r Caz!'

'If you don't come out tonight, I will find your cuzin.'

I couldn't deal with those kinds of threats, so I replied to a couple of the texts before Mark and Sarah called me back inside.

'Really, you shouldn't be smoking at your age,' Mark tutted disapprovingly, swatting the air around me as if to wave away any lingering smoke.

'No, well, if you must, then please do not smoke inside the house,' Sarah added. 'We don't allow smoking in the house. In fact, let's establish some ground rules now so we get off to the best possible start. Now, Mark and I both work during the week at a local charity so we're out of the house at nine a.m. every morning and we'll be locking the door, so I expect you'll be up by then and off to school? I don't know which bus you have to catch but I suppose you'll be able to work that one out, won't you? June says you're in the middle of your GCSEs. Hard work, isn't it?'

I shrugged.

'Well, anyway . . .' she went on. 'We can't leave you in the house on your own. I'm usually back by around three-ish, or sometimes a little earlier, and I can let you in any time from then. There's plenty of food here so do help yourself but please tidy up after you've used the kitchen, and if you could try to keep the bathroom clean too, we would appreciate it. Curfew is ten p.m. sharp every night. Is that alright, Cassie? Can we agree to those rules, do you think?'

I just stared at her, blankly. A curfew at 10 p.m.? It sounded ridiculous to me. My ten-year-old cousin was allowed to stay out later. And the thought of having to be out of the house by nine every morning – why? What did they think I was going to do to their house while they were gone?

'Yeah, fine,' I replied. 'That sounds fine to me.'

Mark and Sarah both grinned with relief. 'Oh good,' she said, then glanced at the clock on the kitchen wall. It was 8.30 p.m. 'Well, it's fairly late now. I expect you'll be wanting to go upstairs and get yourself ready for school tomorrow?'

'Yeah, sure,' I said. 'I think I'll just have a little walk around first though. I don't really know the area.'

'Erm . . . yes, alright,' Mark said, and the pair of them looked at one another uncertainly. Then Sarah added: 'Yes, of course, Cassie. It's not a big place. You do that – have a little wander and we'll see you in a short while.'

I picked up my handbag, put on my denim jacket and headed

for the door. Outside, I saw a familiar car waiting for me. It was Harry. He flashed his lights at me. I got in the car and we drove off.

I don't know what I was expecting from a foster family but staying with Mark and Sarah wasn't anything like I imagined it would be. Kind as they were, they didn't seem to welcome me into their 'family' at all. I wasn't invited to join in their meals, and even when they made tea for each other they rarely asked if I wanted one too. They had no knowledge of my life up till now and seemed to show little interest in what I was doing at school. Actually, I had stopped going to school after that last disastrous exam, not that they knew that. They expected me to live a life completely independent of them, which included making all my own meals and being out of the house while they were at work. One afternoon they had a family barbeque in the garden, to which I was definitely not invited. Sarah informed me that morning: 'We've got our daughter and her children coming round this afternoon for a barbeque lunch so you might want to go out with one of your friends today.'

In other words, I should make myself scarce. Funnily enough, I didn't have any plans for that afternoon. It was such a lovely day and I found myself at one end of the garden, smoking and soaking up the sun, as I watched the family at the other end, standing round the barbeque, enjoying their food. Just seeing them all talking and laughing together made me feel lonelier and sadder than I had in a long time. This was a proper family, of course – a really nice family that got together for summer barbeques in their garden. Kids played on their bikes and the adults shared glasses of wine. It was a great family. And one I wasn't any part of.

Of course, I didn't spend much time there anyway because the men I had been hanging out with before found me straight away. Harry came to collect me the very night I had been dropped off, and we went back to the Convert's for a smoke and a chill. Since then I had been at Mark and Sarah's only for the odd night, as my nights were once more a blur of drugs, men and hotel rooms. If I went back to Sowerby Bridge, it was to have a shower and change before going out again. In truth, nothing had changed in my life at all.

At first, Mark and Sarah had politely asked who it was I was seeing and staying out with till the early hours. They had CCTV outside the house, they explained. They had seen me getting into cars.

'We've seen those men who pick you up,' Sarah said, her brow furrowed in concern. 'Men considerably older than yourself. Who are they?'

'They're just friends,' I'd said.

'But you go out all night long,' Sarah had objected. 'That's not appropriate for a girl your age. You should come home at night to sleep. Where on earth are you sleeping?'

'A friend's house,' I lied. 'It gets late so sometimes it's easier if I stay over.'

'Well, we don't want you staying over at friends' houses, especially if we don't know where you are. We've had to report you missing twice this week already!'

'Sorry about that,' I mumbled.

'We have rules for a reason, Cassie. They're not for our benefit. The rules are there for you – to protect you and keep you safe. How can we keep you safe if we don't know where you are for days at a time? We are responsible for you, we are *in loco parentis*, which means we have taken on the parental duty to look after you, and so we must know where you are at night. Is that clear? We don't want to give you a hard time but we can't do our job properly if you're not here. Please do try to stick to the curfew and then this is going to be so much easier for us all.'

Rules. Curfew. Those words didn't mean much to me. It had got to the point where I had very little control over what happened to me from one moment to the next. If I told any of the men I was with that I had to be home by 10 p.m. they'd just laugh. When I asked to be dropped home, the reply was always the same: 'Later, later.' And of course 'later' meant MUCH later. Days later sometimes. I wasn't even surprised any more when I got into a car and heard the *ka-thunk* of the locks. Sometimes they told me where I was going, sometimes they didn't bother. I didn't have choice in my life. I had no power or control. But as long as someone had a drink, a smoke and some drugs, I didn't much care where I was going or how long for. I took whatever they offered me, so I was out of it for a lot of the time and then, on some occasions, they'd drop me home two or three days later. I was in hotels, in houses, in towns and cities all over the country. I had no idea where I was from one day to the next. How the hell was I meant to get back to Sowerby Bridge for 10 p.m. every night? It was ridiculous.

One evening Ti picked me up with his friend and offered me a pre-rolled joint. When I passed it to him and his mate, they both said no, which was strange, but I didn't really think much of it at the time. So I smoked the whole thing myself as we drove to a hotel. But by the time we got there, I started to feel really weird – not stoned as I expected, but fearful and paranoid. Whatever had been in that joint was very powerful and it made me feel weak and afraid.

That night we got a room and drank a bit before Ti turned on the shower. Then he undressed me and forced me to shower while he watched and talked to his friend in Urdu. Once I'd dried myself, he picked up my underwear and, smiling, told me to put them back on.

Now I was crying – *No, I don't want this. I don't want him to do this to me but I have no choice.* I felt so weak; there had been something strange in that joint. Something that took all the strength from my body. Even though I was crying he held me down and he and his friend took it in turns to have sex with me. I hated every minute. He knew I didn't want this, he could see my tears, but he didn't stop. He was enjoying it.

'Where have you been?'

Pete came to the house one afternoon, after I'd been missing for three days. 'Your foster parents reported you missing again. This is the sixth time, Cassie, in three weeks.'

'I was in Rochdale,' I said. 'I went to see a friend there.' Suddenly I winced in pain and my hand flew to my side.

'What's wrong?' Pete asked.

'Nothing, it's nothing,' I insisted.

'Where does it hurt, Cassie?'

'It's nothing.'

'Cassie? What happened?'

'I was at a friend's house and we got into a fight, that's all. I think my ribs are a bit bruised.'

Pete took a closer look at my left hand, wrapped around my ribcage, and he gently peeled back my sleeve to reveal some ugly marks along my wrists. Purple and reddish bruises swept up from the bottom of my hands towards my elbow, as well as big, fat thumbprints. I knew what they were from but I couldn't tell him.

He asked over and over again but I just shook my head. No, I couldn't tell him. And I couldn't even say why. They'll kill me, I thought to myself. They'll kill me if I tell anyone. That's what they'd said. And not just me, my family too. So I couldn't tell Pete how the men I had been with had pinned my arms above my head and held me down while they took turns raping me. Pete tried his best but I wouldn't say anything more. After a while he sat back in the armchair and rubbed his face with his hand. I sensed the resignation in his voice as he spoke. 'Cassie, this isn't working, is it? This isn't helping you at all.'

My throat grew tight and I shook my head.

'I think we need to think about a different placement, some-where much further away this time,' Pete went on. 'Somewhere they can't find you.'

By the beginning of July, less than a month after I had started living with my foster carers, I had been reported missing nine times. Mark and Sarah were nice but they never stood a chance. They were like the caretakers of a burning building. They swept the corridors as fires blazed around them. They kept trying to impose curfews, telling me to stick to the rules, giving me warnings, and 'groundings' and final warnings. And final *final* warnings. But whatever they said just went over my head. I never argued with them – that wasn't my way. I've never liked confrontation or people getting angry so, whatever they said, I just agreed with them. They just didn't realise I had no choice any more. Even if they gave me the easiest of rules I couldn't hope to stick to them because it wasn't up to me.

It wasn't like being in a real family anyway. They had given me a roof over my head, but that felt like the extent of their caring. They did it because it was their job, their duty, and I didn't get any sense that they wanted to help me in any other way. I slept and showered at their house and that was it. I was still trapped in the same situation and I couldn't escape. Pete said they were going to work on moving me to a different foster placement, but they needed my dad's consent to move me out of the area completely.

I tried to go home to see my family – I knew there might not be much time left together. Occasionally I went round to Marie's place, and she always seemed pleased to see me, but Marie struggled with her own problems and I worried that I was just another headache for her. Knowing I would soon be moving away for good, I asked to go back home to see Dad and Tammy, but Dad wasn't having it. That's when he beat me round the head with the rolled-up newspaper and accused me of destroying the family. There was nothing left in Halifax for me any more.

In mid-July I went to the Convert's house with Harry and told him I would soon be moving out of the area.

'Where are you going?' he asked.

'I don't know,' I replied, frowning. 'They won't tell me, but I think it's pretty far. Maybe Manchester or something.'

Harry took a long drag on his joint and then blew the smoke upwards towards the ceiling. 'I'm not worried. I'll still find you,' he said. 'Wherever they take you, I'll still be able to find you.'

I wondered for a moment if this was true. 'You might not,' I replied. 'My dad's signed the papers. It means they can put me under the care of another local authority. That could be anywhere in the country. It might be too far away.'

Harry sat silently, thinking for a few minutes. Then he got up. 'I've got to get a lighter,' he said, and left the room. He returned a few moments later, closely followed by the Convert.

'You have to pay him,' said Harry, nodding towards the Convert. 'For using his house all this time. You have to give him money.'

'No. Why should I pay him?' I replied. 'Anyway, I haven't got any money.'

'Then you'll have to have sex with him, won't you, Caz?' And he then bent down and started to stroke my head. I didn't like this, it felt creepy.

The Convert moved towards me and asked Harry, 'Is it okay, yeah?'

At that moment, Harry, who was kneeling beside me, grabbed hold of my hands and pulled me down to the floor. The Convert pulled down his trousers and got on top of me and had sex with me. I looked away, concentrating hard on the cracks in the wall as his body pumped up and down on mine. It felt like it went on forever but it must have lasted only a few minutes and then it was all over. He got off and went downstairs. As soon as he was gone, Harry let go of my hands. I was crying but he didn't say anything. I pulled up my clothes and left the house. I was shaking as I walked down the road. It never occurred to me that he would do anything like that after all this time. Harry was my friend, I trusted him. I thought the Convert was a good man, a kind man. I had met his children! All this time he had been so quiet and gentle. I stopped by the side of the road and my stomach heaved. Then I was sick.

A week later, Pete and June came to get me. They said I was being moved to a new foster placement some distance away and that we had a long journey ahead. So this was it. A hundred different emotions ran through me at once – mainly relief, but also fear. I was going into the unknown and I had no idea what my future looked like. Part of me wanted to get away from all the men and the drugs, but I was scared too of being so far away from my family, away from everyone and everything I knew. It was 22 July 2011 and I had been at Mark and Sarah's for six weeks in total – during that time I had been reported missing thirteen times, sometimes for several days at a time. I felt no closer to them on leaving than I had when I'd turned up on their doorstep a few weeks earlier. We were all still strangers. There was no emotional farewell, no hugs or kisses; just a curt little nod from Sarah and a handshake from Mark. A strange, awkward sort of goodbye. I think we all felt disappointed by our time together but no one said anything. They'd stood side by side at the front door, waving as the car took me to my new family. For a brief second I wondered if they were relieved I was going . . . then we turned the corner, and they were gone.

The miles of road disappeared behind us and the same questions went round and round in my head:

Where am I going? What will happen when I get there?

Will everything change?

Will the men find me still?

What will my next foster family be like?

I was desperate for a fresh start, a new life, a normal life. And I knew this was my last chance, my only chance.

God, I hope it works.

PART 2

AFTER

'The clock is running. Make the most of today. Time waits
for no man. Yesterday is history. Tomorrow is a mystery.
Today is a gift. That's why it is called the present.'
Alice Morse Earle

14.

Freedom

STILLNESS. PEACE. I SAT upstairs in my new bedroom and let the thoughts and feelings wash over me. There were no text messages to interrupt my thoughts, no calls to force me out of the house. There was nowhere to go and nothing for me to do. It had been so long since I had just stayed indoors for a night, or had any time to myself, that to begin with all I wanted to do was sit still and stay quiet. I had a lot on my mind. In the past few years my head had been so muddled up I couldn't think at all. My mind went back over the last year and how I had pinballed from one place to another without any sense of permanence. I thought about my dad and what he had said to me before I left. I thought about my sisters and I thought too about my mum. Now, in the peacefulness of my new home, and without the daily diet of drink and drugs, I could sit back and reflect on everything that had happened to me.

It had stopped. It had all come to a complete stop, and that was really overwhelming. At first, I couldn't quite believe the madness was over. I just didn't think it was possible. After a very long drive, Pete and June announced we were here, in Hastings, where my new foster family lived.

'Where's Hastings?' I had asked.

'It's in the south-east, past London,' said June.

I looked at her blankly.

'East Sussex. Have you heard of Sussex?'

I racked my brains, but no, I didn't know Sussex. I might as well have been on Mars. We drove down a hilly road next to a park and pulled up outside a long, tall house with steps leading up to the front door. Suddenly I had butterflies in my stomach.

'It's okay,' Pete reassured me. 'They're really nice. Don't worry.'

The door was opened by a woman in her forties whose wild, curly brown hair flowed over a floor-length floral dress. She wore a very broad grin and welcomed us in warmly. I stepped through the corridor into a large lounge with high ceilings and curved bay windows. The place had a relaxed, airy feel to it and I immediately felt at home.

'Hi, I'm Adam.' A wiry-looking man with a tanned face and a bald head introduced himself.

'And I'm Sheila,' the woman said, following us into the lounge. 'Sit down, sit down. You've had a heck of a journey, haven't you? I bet you're all tired after that.'

Adam brought in cups of tea while a friendly chocolate Labrador approached me, his tail wagging the back half of his body, and started to lick my hand.

'Oh, don't mind Barney!' Sheila pushed the big dog away. 'Are you alright with animals? Barney's harmless. Just a big old lug!'

I smiled. 'Yeah, I like animals.'

'Good, good. Well, you'll meet the girls later after school. Last few days before they break up for the summer. Ginny's fifteen so she's had exams this term, just like you. And Danielle is thirteen.'

'You seem like a nice family,' I sighed. 'But I probably won't be staying here more than a couple of hours.'

Adam and Sheila exchanged worried looks and then Adam said, 'Maybe . . . but, well, let's see how it goes.'

June and Pete left after an hour, but not before Pete insisted on taking my mobile phone.

'What do you need that for?' I was reluctant to part with my phone, the last link to my old life.

'It's for evidential purposes,' Pete said.

'But what if I need to call my dad or my sisters? What if my family needs to get in touch with me?'

'Sorry, Cassie. You'll be fine without it. Your dad has the number of Adam and Sheila's house phone, so you can always get in touch with your family on the landline if you need to. Don't worry, I'll call you tomorrow. Okay?'

Sheila showed me to my bedroom at the top of the Victorian three-storey house. It was a lovely old home with real wooden floorboards, smooth oak bannisters and stained windows above each bedroom door. My room was painted white with long grey curtains at the windows and a big black cast-iron fireplace. The late afternoon sun streamed in, lighting up the room with a pale, peachy glow.

'Oh, this is beautiful!' I exclaimed, as I walked into the bright airy space. I looked out of the window – I could see right over the tops of the trees in the park and out towards the sea. Somewhere, not too far away, seagulls cawed loudly to one another.

'It's a nice room, isn't it?' Sheila smiled. 'You've got this upstairs totally to yourself but you'll have to share a bathroom with the girls down on the next floor, I'm afraid. Now, let's get you sorted out, shall we?'

I hauled my two carrier bags onto the large white dressing table and Sheila helped me unpack. She pulled out the bottles of vodka.

'Well, these two are empty,' she said brightly. 'I'll take them downstairs to put in the recycling.' She then found the third one, which was still half full. 'Okay, erm, why don't we put this one in the medicine cabinet in the bathroom and then, if you feel you need a drink, we'll give you some. Does that sound reasonable?'

I nodded. There wasn't much stuff to put away in the large chest of drawers – just some clothes, my make-up and hair straighteners. I sat down on the bed and suddenly my stomach yawned with hunger. I realised that I hadn't actually eaten yet that day.

'I'm starving,' I said. 'Can I get something to eat?'

Sheila nodded. 'Of course, my love. I've got a nice lasagne for dinner tonight but why don't you go for a quick walk to Morrisons with Adam and get yourself a little snack. Give you a chance to stretch your legs.'

So Adam and I walked to Morrisons, just a few minutes up the road. I smoked a cigarette while he told me a little bit about the area. Once at the supermarket, I chose a tuna and cucumber sandwich.

'You look like you need that!' Adam laughed as I chewed my way through it on the way home.

'I haven't eaten today,' I explained. 'By the way, am I allowed to smoke in the garden?'

'Yeah, course you can,' Adam said. 'This is your home now. No smoking in the house, of course, but please do make use of the garden. It's not much to look at, I'm afraid. Neither Sheila nor I have particularly green fingers, but we do try our best with the pots.'

Adam showed me into the garden through a side gate. It was a lovely courtyard garden and the plants arranged along the walls were in full summer bloom – pretty pink begonias sat in big green pots next to pillar-box red geraniums. There were stone steps with iron railings that led up to the back door of the house, so I took a seat on the steps and lit a fag, admiring the work Adam and Sheila had put into making this place so nice and tranquil. I recognised a few herbs in the beds along the back wall; there was rosemary, parsley and mint. In the centre of the courtyard was a white, cast-iron table and chairs, and in the centre of the table Adam had thoughtfully placed an ashtray for me. It was a kind touch.

For the rest of the afternoon I just sat in my new room, staring out over the rooftops, enjoying the calm and tranquillity of the house. That evening, Sheila and Adam invited me to eat dinner with them. She'd made a hearty lasagne, bubbling over with cheese, and a fresh green salad tossed with oil and vinegar. Seated at the table when I got downstairs were their two daughters, Ginny and Danielle, each dressed in the black skirt and white shirt of their school uniforms. They seemed very smart and well-behaved to me. Their skirts didn't ride up to their bums, but skimmed their knees, and they both wore their straight brown hair in sensible ponytails. They introduced themselves enthusiastically and, as we sat down to eat, the family asked me a little bit about myself. Though shy, I felt their warmth and interest in me was genuine, so I told them all about my own family in Halifax. How my mum had died from Huntington's, and all about my two sisters and my niece Dara. I said I was missing them already.

'My dad's still around,' I added. 'But we don't really get on.'

Sheila explained that she worked in a nursery while Adam worked in an old people's home and this was their first foster placement.

'So, I know this is all new to you, Cassie, and you've come a long way from your family and everything you knew up in Halifax. But we're new to fostering too. So, in a way, we're all in it together and we'll just try our best to make it all work.'

'Okay.' I grinned.

Nobody talked about rules or curfews that night. The girls did the washing up and then the family invited me to sit down with them to watch TV together.

'Do you like *Downton Abbey*?' Ginny asked. 'We love it!'

'I've never heard of it,' I replied.

'Really?' Danielle seemed shocked. 'It's literally all anyone talks about in my class! What do you like to watch, then?'

'Erm . . . I don't know.' I couldn't remember the last time I had sat down and watched TV in the evening. 'I used to watch *Corrie* but I haven't in a while. Um, I don't really watch TV.'

Sheila put a kindly arm around my shoulder. 'Well, you can sit and watch this silly drama with us if you like, but you don't have to. Just do whatever makes you happy.'

'I think I might go to my room, if that's okay?' I said. 'I'm pretty tired.'

'Yes, yes, of course you are! But if you change your mind and want to come down, do join us. I couldn't bear to think of you sitting up there feeling lonely, okay?'

That first night, I had sat on my bed fully dressed until nearly midnight, fully expecting the knock on the door or the beep of a car horn to signal that the men had found me. I had waited, holding my breath, not quite believing that it could possibly be over. In fact, nobody came for me that night, the following night or the night after that. It was astonishing. There was nobody out there when I went to take the dog for a walk in the park opposite – no men waiting for me in cars, nobody at all. Even so, I was always on my guard, nervously looking over my shoulder to check I wasn't being followed on foot or if there was a car cruising nearby. Each time I left the house I felt a flicker of nerves as I opened the front door, expecting to see a man's face on the other side. But it never appeared. They were coming for me, I was sure of it, so I couldn't let my guard down. Even after a couple of weeks, I was still warily looking over my shoulder every time I left the house.

The family were lovely – so warm and down to earth. Sheila loved to cook and made wonderful family meals most nights from scratch: spaghetti Bolognaise, stir-fried rice, big hearty salads, and on Sundays she did a full Sunday roast with all the trimmings. I felt guilty to begin with because I couldn't eat much. I don't know why but I didn't have much of an appetite, and Sheila would look at me over the dinner table apologetically after I put my knife and fork together.

'You didn't like it?' she'd ask plaintively.

'Yes, I did. It was lovely. I'm just . . . I'm not really that hungry today.'

The girls were friendly, and after their school term ended they invited me to the beach every day for a swim. I liked to walk along the shoreline to the spot where they swam but it wasn't always warm enough for me to get into the sea. I'd stand on the edge of the stony beach, shivering, as they dived in, the dog splashing in the shallows.

'Aren't you coming in?' they'd call back to me on the shore.

'It's too cold!' I'd laugh.

'Come on, Cassie!' They'd try to cajole me but I'd shake my head. I didn't mind just sitting there, looking out to sea; it was a lovely way to spend an hour. I'd put a towel down on the stones and just let my mind wander. We went to the gym together too. They were members of a large gym up the road from the house and they all went together as a family two or three times a week. At first I didn't really know what to do, but Ginny showed me how to use the machines and I found that I enjoyed going on the running machine, the cross-fit trainer and the rowing machine. It was the first time I'd been to a gym in my life and I found that I enjoyed working out, getting fit and feeling good about myself. It gave me confidence about my body that I'd never really had before.

At first I thought I would miss the booze and the drugs, but I got through the first day without a drink and felt fine, so I didn't really think about having a drink after that. After a while, I forgot the vodka was even in the medicine cupboard. I missed the weed more. It was strange not being able have a smoke at night to relax. It was all I'd ever known for so long, and now I was straight for the first time in years. It was a hard adjustment. Quite often, the family invited me to watch a movie with them in the evenings, something I found difficult. Just sitting still and concentrating on a film for more than an hour was a challenge. I was always jumping up, popping out to have a fag or going upstairs to my room.

I wanted to be polite so I was careful to ask before I did anything. Sometimes, they were surprised about this.

'Can I take a biscuit please?' I asked Adam one evening.

'It's just a biscuit,' Ginny said, grinning at me. 'Why would you ask to take a biscuit?'

'Well, if I was at my dad's house, I'd have to ask or he'd hit me,' I explained.

Her face fell. 'Oh, right. Well, you don't have to worry. No one's going to hit you here.'

I was reassured but, even so, I kept forgetting that the family were very relaxed about that sort of thing and I didn't want to upset anybody, so I tried to remember my manners and help out as much as I could around the house. In truth, I was very grateful to Adam and Sheila and I just wanted to show my appreciation. I had no doubt whatsoever that moving in with them had probably saved my life.

In-mid August, June came down for a meeting and I told her that I was getting on well with Adam and Sheila and I'd like to stay. 'Anyway,' I said, 'there's nothing left for me in Halifax.' Adam and Sheila agreed that the placement was going well and felt I had made good progress since my arrival.

'Cassie's got excellent caring skills,' Sheila noted. 'She likes children and she's always offering to help out. I think, because of her experience looking after her mum, she might do well on a childcare course. What do you think, Cassie? Would you be interested in starting college in September? We'll help you find a suitable course.'

'Yeah, I'd really like that,' I said. 'But do you think I'd get a place? I haven't got any GCSEs.'

'Don't worry about that,' Sheila said. 'You're a very bright girl and I think you'd do well if you started a foundation course. Adam and I can help you with all the forms.'

I went red with embarrassment. Nobody had ever told me I was bright before. It was so nice to hear her say that, and I was so happy for the chance to study at college. I had missed out on so much already – living with Ginny and Danielle made that clear to me. I hadn't had a childhood at all. Now I longed for everything I'd missed out on – the chance at a normal life, a proper education and maybe even a job at the end of it all.

I was into a routine now for the first time in years and it felt good. I got up, went to the beach, filled in some forms, walked the dog, tidied my room and went to the gym a couple of times a week. The rest of the time I helped Sheila with the cooking – she taught me how to make some of her best meals, and I spent time in the garden or just sitting upstairs in my bedroom, thinking about the past and reflecting on everything.

I had a lot to think about and, at first, I couldn't share my thoughts with anyone. I couldn't even make sense of them myself. Sometimes, when I was out, my heart would start to beat faster and I'd suddenly feel very frightened for no reason. *I have to get home, I have to get home* . . . the same thought would go round and round in my head and, until I was back in the house, nothing could calm me down. I had nightmares too. They had started shortly after my arrival. Now that I was getting a proper night's sleep, instead of just passing out from drugs, I was having proper dreams. And in those dreams I was back in the cars again, or locked in a hotel room, and the men were all around me. I'd wake up, bathed in sweat, panting and gripped by fear. In my rational mind, I knew it was over, I knew they couldn't find me again, but the thoughts and dreams still haunted me.

But generally I was happy. For the first time in years I was happy and free. I could do what I liked, I could go out when I wanted to or just stay in the house and listen to my music. Dad called a couple of times, and he promised to come down and see me, but he never did. I was half disappointed but also a little relieved too. He was my only parent now but he was also a large part of my troubled past, and though I wanted to forgive and move on, it made me angry whenever I thought about the way he had treated me. Did I even want him to come and see me? I wasn't sure. Leaving Halifax had been hard but I knew this was the best thing that had ever happened to me and I didn't want to look backwards.

True to their word, Sheila and Adam helped me get all the paperwork done to start a Health and Social Care foundation course at college at the beginning of September. I was nervous at first, particularly about talking to the other students. I realised my accent was different from other people's and I was worried how I would explain being down in Hastings when I came from West Yorkshire.

'Don't worry about that,' Sheila said. 'Lots of people in Hastings come from all over the country, so it's not unusual for you to have a different accent. Just be yourself – be friendly and, if people ask, you tell them what you feel like telling them. I'm sure you'll find it easy to make friends. You're a really nice girl.'

Their words, their constant love and support, boosted my confidence enormously and, by mid-September, merely eight weeks after I had arrived in Hastings, I was enrolled on a college course, looking towards a bright new future. It was everything I'd ever wanted. They treated me just like their own daughter and I felt like I had finally found a wonderful family, the family I'd always wanted. Nobody took drugs, nobody drank or gambled or stayed out for days at a time. Nobody hit me or threatened me or gave me a hard time. I was treated with love and respect at all times. And yet, and yet . . . the memories never went away. They were always there, lurking at the back of my mind, bubbling just below the surface, threatening to overtake me at any moment and engulf me with fear and panic. It didn't take much to set me off. Sometimes, just seeing a group of Asian men in the street was enough to make me feel threatened and upset. I tried to not let it affect me too much but there were times I just wanted to run and hide.

Then, one day, a couple of weeks after starting college, I saw it. I saw the article in the newspaper. And that changed my life for ever.

15.

Awakening

'It is alleged that the girl was a victim of Child Sexual Exploitation since the age of 15, being given drugs, cigarettes, alcohol and food in exchange for sex with men, sometimes up to five at a time. This exploitation went on for many months, with the victim being expected to have sex with many men that she didn't know. At first she was unaware of the abuse and was too ashamed to reveal what was happening to her. Finally, after she was arrested for smashing up the counter in a takeaway shop, the girl revealed her plight to the police.'

My heart thudded in my chest as I read the words over and over again. It was a report in the newspaper about some men who had been arrested in Rochdale as part of an investigation into something called Child Sexual Exploitation. This girl's experiences sounded frighteningly similar to my own, and I reached for my phone to look up Child Sexual Exploitation online. The definition read: 'Child Sexual Exploitation (CSE) is a type of sexual abuse. Children in exploitative situations and relationships receive something such as gifts, money or affection as a result of performing sexual activities or others performing sexual activities on them.'

That was me! That is exactly what happened to me.

I got fags, booze and drugs and they took what they wanted from me in exchange. It was a form of abuse. I couldn't believe it. Why had no one spoken to me before about CSE? Why had I been accused of being involved in prostitution? I pored over that newspaper report for ages, examining the details of the case. It was all so familiar. My heart went out to this girl and, at the same time, I felt quiet admiration for her, for having the courage to speak to the authorities.

It was September 2011 and I'd been at college for two weeks. The newspaper had been lying open on the kitchen table when my eye was drawn to the report about the case in Rochdale, just outside of Manchester. Rochdale wasn't even that far from where I'd grown up in Halifax. In fact, I had been there one time with a friend called Jemma. She had invited me to go with her and her boyfriend – an Asian man in his thirties called Mick. We went to a flat above a takeaway shop and met another guy there who had vodka and weed.

That night, Mick took Jemma to a bedroom in the flat and they had sex, but then he wanted her to have sex with someone else and she wouldn't, so they ended up having a big row and she walked out. I followed her out, but I couldn't find her and I had no credit on my phone to call her. I'd never been to Rochdale before, so I had no idea where to look, and I ended up going back to the flat. I was surprised to find that there were several more men there by the time I got back. I asked them to drop me back to Halifax but they refused and I didn't have any money to pay for a cab. After that, things went a bit hazy and the next thing I knew I was in the back seat of a car and some guy was all over me, kissing me and touching me. I asked them what time it was and they said about four in the morning. I asked them what had happened but nobody would answer me – they just talked among themselves in their own language.

I was dropped back in Halifax in the early hours and, as I got out, I realised I didn't have a bra on. Now I read about the case in the paper and all the men who had been arrested looked like the men who had abused me. They were all Pakistani. It was like somebody had turned on the lights. All this time I'd been ignorant of what was happening to me, assuming I'd got myself into these situations, that they were of my own making. Every time it happened I just thought it was my fault. Now I realised that I had been abused and exploited and the men I'd been hanging out with, 'chilling' with, weren't really my friends. They were my abusers. My hands shook and I felt myself breathing hard. I was upset, but also angry. Very angry.

I found Sheila in the lounge, doing the ironing with the TV on in the background.

'Sheila, can I speak to you a minute?' I asked. I clearly looked upset because Sheila immediately put down the iron, turned off the TV and came over.

'Of course, Cassie, what is it? What's wrong?'

I showed her the article. 'This is what happened to me,' I said, my voice trembling. 'It was the same thing – Child Sexual Exploitation.' I was careful to say the words properly. It was the first time I had uttered those words but I knew for a fact it wouldn't be the last. I suddenly had a name for the unspeakable things that had been done to me. I didn't yet know how it all fitted together but I felt sure this was important.

'Oh, Cassie.' Sheila looked crestfallen. She took the article and led me back to the kitchen where we sat down together across the large oak table.

'Tell me,' she said. 'What happened?'

'There were lots of men, and they all had my number, so they would call me and text me all the time, asking if I wanted to go out for a drink and a smoke. I was bombarded by calls all the time and if I didn't respond they would get pissed off and call me nasty names. It was like being stalked. They gave me booze and the drugs for free, except . . . except it wasn't free, was it? I mean, they made me think I owed them something so that's how I ended up having sex with lots of them. I was always so drunk or out of it that I couldn't really say no. I couldn't speak.'

'Cassie . . .' Sheila reached out a hand to mine and held it there. 'It wasn't your fault. You were just a child.'

'I thought they were my friends!' I erupted. 'I feel so stupid. I thought they liked me. They always said nice things to me, like I had nice eyes and I was really pretty. But it just got worse and worse. They'd pick me up in their cars and, you know, at first I liked having somewhere to go and people to talk to at night. I didn't like being at home much. But by the end, I really didn't have any choice. They said I had to go with them. Then I'd be taken to a hotel or someone's house, and by then I'd have had a lot to drink and probably pills or coke or something and . . . well, you know, they'd take turns . . .'

I stared at my hands resting on the table. I couldn't look at Sheila, it was too humiliating. How many times had it happened? I had lost count of the number of occasions I had woken from a drug-induced stupor to find a complete stranger having sex with me.

'I didn't know them,' I said quietly. 'I didn't know their names or anything about them. Five or ten in one night, sometimes more. I was so ashamed of myself. I'm ashamed now.'

'It's not your fault, Cassie . . . really, you have to believe me. They were grown-ups and you were just a child.'

I was silent for a moment, thinking back to all the times I'd been offered 'a drink and a chill'. I always thought they were helping me, giving me drink and drugs for free, but it always ended the same way, with me flat on my back, crying, while a man fucked me.

'Cassie, this is really serious,' Sheila said thoughtfully. 'Do you want to talk to the social worker about what happened? Maybe the police?'

Did I want to talk to the police? It was a terrifying thought – of going to the police with all the information I had. I was scared of remembering what had happened, scared of bringing it all up again. For so long I had tried to hide from the truth, first by taking drugs and then, down here in Hastings, I thought I had escaped it all and could start a new life. But the nightmares had never gone away and the panic attacks still found me. Worse, the men were still out there! It was true that I had escaped, but what about all the girls left in Halifax? What about Dara? If they were free to abuse other girls, what would stop them from approaching my niece? Nothing, nothing at all.

'Yes,' I said. 'I want to talk to someone about it. Pete. I'll talk to Pete.'

For so long I had pushed the memories to the back of my mind, trying to block out the truth of what had happened to me. Now, for the first time, I had a name for it – Child Sexual Exploitation – and just being able to call it something, to identify it as a form of abuse, allowed me to let the memories back in. June came down from Halifax shortly after my chat to Sheila and I told her that I was ready to speak to the police about what had happened to me. A new social worker was appointed to me, a woman called Anna, from Calderdale, and she seemed very kind and sympathetic. I told her a little bit about the men who had abused me, but it was just the tip of the iceberg – there were so many encounters, so much had happened, I hardly knew where to begin.

'It was happening every day,' I explained. 'The men all seemed to know who I was and they called me and texted me all the time. I was hounded day and night. It was constant. Whenever I left the house, someone was there waiting for me. My life wasn't my own any more. I was trapped.'

'Did any of them use protection, do you know?' Sheila asked gently.

'No, not that I can remember.'

At that point Sheila and Anna exchanged a look.

'Well, Cassie, it might be an idea to visit the sexual health clinic in town,' Sheila said. 'Just to get some tests because it's better to find out now if you've caught something. The sooner you find out, the sooner you can get treated.'

'Yes, I think that's a good idea,' Anna said.

Fear pricked my skin. 'You mean, tests for sexual diseases?' I asked. I didn't know anything about sexual diseases, although I'd heard of HIV and I knew you could get that from unprotected sex. I also knew it could be fatal if it developed into AIDS. I was scared now.

'I'm sure everything's fine,' Sheila tried to reassure me. 'But as I say, it's best to find out for certain.'

So, one morning in late October, Sheila accompanied me to the Sexually Transmitted Infections (STI) clinic inside the local hospital and I was tested for a number of different things like Chlamydia, Herpes, Syphilis and HIV. I felt so worried and scared, and when the nurse asked me lots of questions for her form, I could barely get the words out. She assured me that she was not there to judge and that all the answers were completely confidential. They were simply necessary in order for the clinicians to work out how best to advise and support me.

'Do you have any symptoms?' she asked kindly, scanning the form in front of her.

'No,' I said.

'Have you been sexually active in the last year?'

'Yes.'

'Are your partners known or unknown?'

'Er . . . erm . . . unknown.'

'How many sexual partners have you had over the past year?'

I was stumped. I had no idea. I felt like bursting into tears and running out of there but Sheila took my hand and gave it a reassuring squeeze.

'She doesn't know,' she answered for me. 'Multiple. She's been a victim of abuse.'

'Oh, okay.' The nurse looked up briefly, apologetically. 'I'm really sorry, Cassie. This isn't meant to upset you. I've just got to answer these questions. Did you or your partners use any form of contraception?'

I shook my head.

'Okay, that's it. No more questions.' The nurse smiled and closed her folder. 'Let's get your tests done and then we'll try and have the results to you within a fortnight.'

The next two weeks I tried to stay busy at college and I did actually make some new friends from my class. Everyone was very friendly and I was pleased that nobody made a big deal out of the fact that I was from Yorkshire. At nights I went to the gym or met some of my new friends in town. But later, alone in bed, when I turned out the lights, the worries came flooding in. *What if I have HIV? What then?* It was a terrifying thought and as much as I tried not to think about it, it preyed on my mind. How many people had I had sex with in the past year? I couldn't answer that question even if I wanted to. There had been so many – and so many I didn't know about.

Two weeks later my mobile rang when I was on my way to the gym.

'Cassie Pike? I'm calling from the STI clinic with your results.'

My stomach flipped over and I held my breath. 'Yes?'

'We have a positive result for gonorrhoea. Do you know what that is?'

'No.'

'Okay, well, it's nothing to worry about – a bacterial infection – but you will need to get a course of antibiotics to treat it. We'll get a prescription for you and you can pick that up from the clinic over the next few days.'

'Okay, thank you. Is, erm, is that it?'

'Yes, that's all. The rest of your results were negative.'

The call ended and my heart was still thumping madly. Part of me felt utterly disgusted that I'd got an infection from one of the men and that I'd had it all this time without even knowing. On the other hand, I was massively relieved that I didn't have HIV. There was no doubt about it – it could have been far worse.

In the end it was fairly easy to kill the infection with antibiotics; it was far harder to shake the revulsion from knowing that one of those men had given it to me. I felt dirty and unclean and I became obsessive about washing. Pete came down in early December and we talked a little. He said he would start the formal video interviews with me early the following year.

'I knew you were in trouble really early on,' he admitted to me. 'There were so many times I tried to help but it was really difficult. My hands were tied. I'm just so pleased you're doing well now.'

'I'm really happy. I feel like I've got a second chance, I really do. But that doesn't mean they've stopped abusing other girls, does it? I just want to stop them doing it to anyone else,' I said.

'What happens if they find another girl to do it to? I was eleven when they started with me. Dara's ten now. Her family is a mess, her dad's now in prison and my sister struggles to get through the day. She seems really vulnerable. I worry about her all the time.'

'We'll do our best,' Pete said. 'All you have to do is talk to us, tell us what happened. Are you sure you want to go ahead with this?'

I nodded.

'I'll be there for your interviews,' said Anna. 'Sheila and I will come with you, and if at any time you feel too upset to carry on, you just let us know and we'll stop them. The important thing is for you to feel comfortable doing this.'

Christmas with my foster family was like nothing I had experienced before. There was a proper turkey dinner with crispy spuds, fluffy Yorkshire puddings, bread sauce and about fifteen different vegetables. They had bought a real tree for the lounge, and one afternoon the whole family got together to decorate it with an assortment of beautiful glass baubles and wooden ornaments: little wooden sleighs, angels, reindeers and Santas. On top was a white angel made out of paper plates by the girls when they were only young.

'It's the same angel we've had for years,' Sheila laughed. 'It's falling apart but we can't bear to get rid of it.'

There were loads of presents in front the tree and I was surprised and touched to find that many had my name written on the front. I couldn't believe it when I unwrapped my gifts on Christmas day – clothes, toiletries, chocolates and a lovely silver ring with a leaf pattern on it.

'Oh, it's beautiful,' I gasped, as I placed the ring on my finger. I was overwhelmed by their kindness. 'You didn't have to do all this.'

'Nonsense,' said Sheila, her eyes shimmering with tears. 'It's Christmas. You deserve it.'

I wanted to cry. The whole day was bittersweet. Although it was lovely to share this special family Christmas with Sheila, Adam and the girls, it was such a contrast to my previous Christmases. The previous year I had celebrated with a McDonald's Happy Meal and a bottle of vodka. This year I was actually drinking wine out of a proper wine glass, something I had never done before. Before Mum died we had celebrated Christmas with her – first at home and then at her care home. But after she died Dad didn't bother. He said he didn't have any money for presents anyway, so there was no point. It made me so angry now, thinking about my dad, about how little he had given me.

I looked at Ginny and Danielle laughing with their parents, enjoying the silly jokes from the crackers we pulled together, everyone wearing their coloured paper crowns, and for a moment I envied them. I envied the fact that this was all they had ever known – a loving, caring, stable family home where everyone got on. Why had they got this and I got my dad? It felt so unfair. Why had I grown up with a dying mother and a violent, drug-addicted father who only bothered to pay me attention when he was beating the shit out of me? What was that – just plain bad luck? I couldn't work it out. All I knew was that some people had a really nice life while others had to deal with a lot of bad stuff from a really young age. And there didn't seem to be any reason for it.

I made the most of the holidays, spending time with the family as well as my new friends from college. One girl, Hannah, was really nice and she was friends with a bloke called Jake on Facebook. They were always talking over Messenger on her phone, so one day I grabbed the phone off her and started chatting to him myself. He thought this was very funny and we exchanged numbers. Jake seemed down to earth and friendly, and one day in late December we actually met for the first time, outside a chippy near my house. I knew all about Jake already because he'd told me a lot about himself on the phone but we talked more over the next half an hour. He was a dad to two little boys from a previous relationship who lived with him half the week and with his ex for the other half. He was a little bit older than me at twenty-two, and he worked in the construction industry. I got the feeling that Jake was a devoted dad, but he had never planned to be a young father and found that it had isolated him from the group of friends he'd grown up with. I told him that I'd grown up in Halifax and was now living down south because I didn't get on with my dad. I didn't tell him anything more.

We sat in his car for a while, chatting, and straight away I knew I liked him. He was funny and sweet and he talked a lot about his kids and his family. I'd never had a real boyfriend before but I had a feeling that Jake liked me, and when I said I had to get going, he asked if we could meet again.

'Okay,' I agreed shyly.

'Do I get a goodbye kiss?' he asked, as I opened the car door.

'No, not yet.' I grinned and got out. 'Let's just see how it goes.'

Jake was a nice guy, I could tell, but I would not be rushing into a relationship with him. For me, there was too much at stake.

As the year ended, I felt more optimistic than I had in a very long time. On New Year's Eve I had a quick drink with Jake in the first part of the evening and then went home to see in 2012 watching the fireworks on TV with Adam, Sheila and the girls. Surrounded by their warmth and love, I was happier than I had been in years. I was finally on track, heading towards the bright future I had always hoped for but which I had never been able to see clearly. What a change in eighteen months! I now had a loving, supportive family around me, new friends, and I was about to embark on a journey to end the cycle of abuse that had trapped me for so long. It was a scary thought, and I had no idea just how long the journey would be, but one thing I was certain of: I was ready to do it.

16.

The Investigation

ON THE FIRST DAY of my police interviews I was so nervous I spent the entire morning shaking. The police had set up a special interview suite in a house in town where Pete was set to ask me questions in front of a camera. The other police officer would watch the recording from behind a screen in the same room and switch over the recording tapes every forty-five minutes. Anna and Sheila came with me but they weren't allowed to sit in the interview room so they watched the interviews on a screen in the other room. At first it was just me and Pete.

'Right, let's go back and start at the beginning,' Pete said gently. 'Let's start with the first person you met, shall we? Can you remember who that might have been?'

I racked my brains and then it came to me that Ali had been the first guy and it wasn't too hard to talk about Ali, I suppose, because nothing bad had happened with him. He was just the first guy I met who had offered me 'a smoke and a chill'. From that point on, people started to get in touch with me –

they seemed to know who I was and, from there, I met others like Imie 1, Imie 2, Harry, Bilal, Tupac, Maj, Bilal, Goldie and the Convert.

It was really hard to open up about what these men had done to me. At first I stumbled, red-faced, over my short, one-word answers, feeling horribly self-conscious and embarrassed. I had spent so long trying not to even think about these events that saying them out loud was a frightening experience. With Pete watching me, and all those other people looking at me on the screen, I struggled to talk about what had happened. I was so ashamed of it all. But Pete kept gently nudging me on, encouraging me, giving me confidence and letting me know it was okay. And somehow I started to tell him about the abuse.

There were times I really couldn't talk. The words simply wouldn't form themselves in my mouth. I could see the images, recall the feelings and find myself unable to give voice to the terrible events that I was reliving. In those moments, I'd asked for a fag break and then stand outside in the garden, shaking, taking deep drags on my cigarette and trying not to cry. Many times Sheila came and stood with me.

'It's okay. Don't worry, you're doing great,' she'd say, putting a comforting arm around my shoulders. 'Really. You're being so brave. I'm really proud of you.'

'It's hard . . .' I swallowed.

'I can't imagine,' Sheila whispered. 'I mean, I can't imagine how hard this is for you. Do your best, Cassie. That's all you can do. Remember, there is a reason for all this pain. To help catch the men who do it. To get justice.'

'I'm doing it for Dara.'

'Well, think about Dara then. Think about her.'

I held the image of my niece Dara's face in my mind and that gave me the courage to keep going.

The interviews were made more difficult by the fact that there were large chunks of time completely wiped out by the drink and drugs. Pete would ask me questions for which I simply had no answers.

'What was his name?'

'I don't know.'

'Where did he take you?'

'It was a house somewhere. I don't know where it was.'

'Can you remember what the street looked like?'

'Maybe . . . I don't know. I didn't see it properly. It was dark and I was really out of it.'

'What did he look like?'

'Asian, short dark hair, a goatee.'

'Can you remember anything else? Any sort of distinguishing marks at all? Moles, scars, tattoos?'

I shook my head, feeling frustrated and inadequate, not being able to provide more details, but Pete said not to worry and that I was doing really well to remember everything that I did. He said we would get there in the end.

One day, I arrived at the interviewing house and Pete had a list of telephone numbers in front of him.

'These are numbers from the phone we took off you last summer,' he explained. 'There are over a hundred different numbers here from calls and text messages. Have a look.'

He turned the list round to face me and I scanned it for a few seconds.

'Cassie, did you have sex with all those contacts in your phone, do you think?'

I thought back to the people who called and texted me and I knew the answer: 'Yes.'

'All of them?'

'All of them, and probably lots more.'

Pete looked at me for a second longer than usual. I knew he worked hard to be professional, to hide his surprise and shock, but there was no mistaking how he felt. All the way through he had been careful with his reactions, careful not to alarm me or make me feel uncomfortable or judged. He knew I was the victim. He had known before anyone else. And yet that two-second stare had betrayed his real feelings.

I looked at the floor.

'Thank you, Cassie, that's really helpful.'

I wanted to cry.

The interviews took time. A lot of time. To begin with, we were doing around three or four days a week, with each day starting at 9 a.m. and finishing sometime between three and five o' clock in the afternoon. The worst part was seeing the effect my evidence had on everyone around me. It didn't surprise me that Sheila and Anna were upset. Of course, I knew it was upsetting to hear about how I had been abused by so many people – how they had held me down and raped me, how they had disregarded my feelings, hurt my body and ignored my shouts of 'no' – but when the officers, big grown men, started to cry too, I found it really distressing. These were police officers! They had seen and heard a lot of bad stuff in their jobs. They tried not to let it show, of course, swiping quickly at their eyes as if getting rid of a piece of grit. Or coughing and excusing themselves for a comfort break. But I could tell they were crying and their reactions started to bring it home to me how serious this was, just how bad it had been.

Gradually all the jagged pieces of my life started to fit together. Up till now, I had thought of them as a series of one-off experiences, each one separate. I thought I was just unlucky. But Pete was sceptical of the idea that they were coincidences.

'The men were probably passing round your number,' Pete said. 'That's how they knew you. They were linked. These weren't just random men who happened to pass by and pick you up. They were talking to each other, letting others know you were available.'

At the time, I had thought of the guys I hung around with as nice people. It was difficult to imagine that what they were doing was criminal – giving me drink, drugs – but it slowly sunk in that they were doing it deliberately to make it more difficult or even impossible for me to say no. It wasn't kindness, it was selfishness. At the time it had felt so random, the guys stopping me in the street, the messages on my phone, but once I realised that they were in contact with one another, it all made more sense. That was why I was getting messages from people I'd never met, asking to meet up, because they had been given my number by someone else. The men who had picked me off the street weren't 'trying their luck' – they knew who I was all along.

The real problem was that there was so much evidence. Once I began to recall the various events over the past few years, more and more episodes came to the surface. It was like opening the floodgates – once I started talking, I just couldn't stop.

'Is that all?' Pete asked, after several days of interviewing.

I shook my head.

'No, there's more. There's lots more.'

Within the first couple of weeks, Pete said he couldn't carry on doing the interviews because he was too close to the case and was getting very personally involved. Two other police officers took over the interviewing – Richard and Mina – and we carried on. And on and on . . . Apart from my foster family, who were fantastically supportive, I didn't tell anyone what I was doing. I just tried to get on with my life.

I was still going to college and doing the coursework. Meanwhile, I had a proper date with Jake at the end of January, during which I admitted to him that I was in care because of a 'situation' at home. I didn't feel like saying anything more than that. I liked Jake – he was caring, handsome and funny – but I wasn't ready to share my life story with him. Not yet, anyway. We started to hang out more and more and then I went for dinner with him and his family. I met his mum Jeanette, her partner Barry and Jake's brother Owen. They were very nice to me and I even got a friendly lick from the family dog Coco! They had a lovely home and I was pleased that he came from a kind, stable upbringing. It wasn't long before we were a proper couple, seeing each other almost every day, but I wasn't ready to tell him about the work I was doing with the police. It was still too early and, at that point, I wasn't sure where it was all leading. I was only just working it out for myself. I knew that if we carried on seeing each other I would have to confide in him at some point, but not in those early days. I just didn't know what to say.

In March I introduced Jake to my foster family and they invited him over for a Sunday dinner. I wanted them to like him but I was scared that, knowing my past, they wouldn't approve of the fact that he was six years older than me. So we told them we'd met at college where he was doing a catering course. I didn't want to lie to them but I was desperate they accept him. Unfortunately it backfired when Sheila put him on the spot.

'Well, you're the chef, Jake,' she said brightly, after setting down a steaming Sunday roast on the table. 'What's your professional opinion of the food?'

'Oh, it's wonderful, Sheila,' he beamed. 'You're a great cook. The only thing I'd say is that the potatoes are slightly under seasoned. Other than that, terrific.'

And with that he grabbed the salt shaker and poured a massive handful all over his spuds. My eyes nearly popped out of my head when I saw how he had drenched the potatoes in salt, but he just kept smiling and eating. Oh God, it looked horrible! He's going to need a big drink after that, I thought. Although they were wary at first, Sheila and Adam liked Jake a lot and were supportive of our relationship. It wasn't long before I admitted to them that he wasn't actually at college but worked in construction. They laughed when I told them about the salt incident but said they hoped I wouldn't feel under pressure to mislead them again.

Then, about six months into the investigation, there was a

breakthrough. When I first came down to Hastings, I had asked for some of my clothes that were still at my dad's place to be sent on to me. The police had discovered a washing basket full of dirty clothes in my wardrobe and, for some reason, they had been put in a black plastic sack and left with the police. They had never made it down to Hastings, which was something of a stroke of luck because, as Mina explained, they contained vital evidence.

'Cassie, do you remember this underwear?' she asked me, showing me pictures of various pairs of knickers I'd abandoned in the washing basket.

'Yeah, those are my knickers,' I said.

'And could anyone else have worn them after you?' '

'No, they were in my wash basket because I'd worn them. They were dirty.'

'Okay, well, the reason I'm asking is that we took DNA samples from your knickers and we found evidence of six different men's DNA on your underwear. This is really important because it is corroborative evidence of your statements.'

I was so pleased. It was really good to know that the police could back up my claims with DNA evidence. They were also going after CCTV evidence from the hotels I'd been to, as well as text messages and phone calls, but that didn't necessarily prove the men were guilty of raping me. The DNA evidence was hard proof. It gave me a real boost.

By mid-August I felt the time had come to share the truth with Jake about my past. The interviews weren't going away – if anything, the demands of the investigation were growing. I was required to make identifications of the men and, occasionally, the police would take me up to Halifax to identify the places where the abuse had taken place. There were times I had told Jake I was at home but then I failed to answer his messages and it was becoming fairly obvious I had a big secret. I didn't want him to be insecure about our relationship so, one afternoon, when we were on our way his mum's house for lunch, I screwed up all my courage and started to talk.

'Look, Jake, there's been some things going on which I couldn't talk about and you've had to be really patient with me but I think I need to tell you know what's happening. The thing is, I've been scared to tell you because, well, what I have to say is shocking and you might think of me differently afterwards.'

'I won't,' he said quickly. 'I know there are things you find hard to talk about but, well, I love you, Cassie, and nothing you can say can change that. Nothing.'

'The thing is . . . I was a victim of Child Sexual Exploitation from the age of twelve to sixteen and I'm now helping the police to try and prosecute the men involved. That's why you can't get hold of me sometimes. I have to spend a lot of time with the police.'

I held my breath, waiting for a response.

'Right. Okay,' Jake replied slowly, a confused look on his face. 'What's Child Sexual Exploitation? Is that something like child prostitution?'

'It's not prostitution, no. It's abuse. It's sexual abuse of a child by adults and the reason I'm helping the police is because I don't want any more kids to go through what I went through.'

'I see. Was there more than one of them, then?'

'Yes, there were. Quite a lot more than one.'

'Okay. Well, if you're helping to stop it happening, that's a really good thing.'

'So you're okay with it, then?'

'Of course I am,' he said seriously. 'It wasn't your fault. You were just a kid, and like you say, it was abuse.'

I felt so relieved to have finally got this out in the open, though I knew Jake had only the vaguest notion of what I was saying. To be honest, I didn't feel like going into all the details with him. It was just too difficult. But just like he promised, nothing changed between us – he was still as kind and loving and supportive as ever and it was a big relief that he knew what was really going on.

The thing was, I had probably seemed quite innocent to him when we first met. Certainly, I didn't throw myself into a physical relationship. In fact, it took over two months before we went to bed together. I didn't want to rush things and Jake was very patient with me. I'd never experienced feelings for anyone before – and it took me a long time to trust him with them. I had been very passive during the period I had been abused. Sex had been something that was done to me. I'd never taken an active part in it. My relationship with Jake was mutual, loving and passionate. It was different in every single way: I wanted to hold him, I wanted to kiss him, but I was self-conscious and I'm sure Jake, who didn't know my past at all, took that for innocence and inexperience. Considering that I'd made him wait so long when we were seeing each other every day, he must have assumed I was a virgin, and in a way, I was. I felt like a virgin – even though I had slept with over a hundred men, I still felt inexperienced when it came to sex.

The more I talked, the more I remembered. By the beginning of September the investigation was passed to the Homicide and Major Enquiry Team. The police were working on leads involving dozens of men. I realised that if I was going to see this through, I couldn't carry on my Health and Social Care course in college so I dropped out. There simply weren't enough hours in the day and something had to give. Helping the police was like a full-time job – there were so many people involved, and so much evidence. They took me back up to Calderdale and I spent many days driving around town with them, pointing out the various houses and hotels where I'd been taken. Some days the phone rang and I didn't feel up to it. I just didn't feel like talking about the abuse. I was so sick of it all that I didn't want to carry on. The investigation had taken over my life in the same way the CSE had – I couldn't make plans any more or get on with my life. I couldn't stay at college and I couldn't get a job either. My life was on hold. There was always so much they wanted from me and it drained my energy. Sometimes I just wanted to tell them to leave me alone but Jake encouraged me to carry on. On those days I felt stressed and upset, Jake gave me strength.

'This won't go on forever,' he reassured me. 'It'll all be over soon. Remember, if you want justice, you have to do this.'

But it wasn't quick. In the end it took five years to bring the cases to court. During that time there were long periods when I didn't think about the past but then, suddenly, it would all come crashing down on me at once. Knowing that I was the sole witness in so many cases, I'd feel overwhelmed by the responsibility. It was too much and it made me feel helpless and depressed. On top of that, I suffered still from flashbacks and nightmares. They would come without warning, triggered by the most innocent things. Sometimes, just watching a programme featuring a group of Asian men was enough to make my heart start to race. I'd hear their voices and suddenly I'd feel uncomfortable and anxious and want to leave the room. Or driving around in Jake's car at night – that sometimes put me back in that dark time when I had no control over my life. Fear engulfed me. I couldn't breathe. I just wanted to get out of the car and run.

'Please, Jake, take me home,' I'd whisper, as I struggled to control my breathing.

'What's wrong?' he'd ask.

'Bad memories,' I'd reply. 'That's all. Just some bad memories.'

'They're not here,' Jake insisted. 'It's just me. You're safe.'

'I know, I know . . . but please take me home.'

It wasn't easy but I kept going, pushing through those difficult times to try and get on with my life. I was determined not to let my past dictate my future.

17.

Moving On

'I DON'T UNDERSTAND . . .' I looked at my birth certificate, confused and upset. 'It says here my surname is Mallion, my mum's surname, but I've always thought I was a Pike.'

'That's odd. Let's have a look.'

I passed the document to Jake and he scanned it from top to bottom.

'It doesn't even have your dad's name on it,' he said. 'Look, in the section where you usually put the father's name, it's been left blank.'

'What does that mean?' I wondered aloud. 'Why isn't my dad on my birth certificate?'

'Don't know.' Jake shook his head. 'Maybe it's something to ask your dad. Or your sisters.'

I had requested that the police send down my birth certificate from Halifax during the time I was applying for my college course, but it had taken them ages to locate it and when it did eventually arrive, I had already been through my first year of college. The problem was, it didn't say what I thought it should say. The name on the certificate was completely different to the one I had used all my life. I had always assumed I was a Pike, like my dad and my sisters, but I was actually Cassie Mallion. Bizarre. Why on earth did I have Mum's surname and why wasn't Dad on the certificate? It was baffling but, as Jake suggested, I asked my sister Tammy for an answer.

'It's because Mum had an affair,' Tammy said bluntly when I explained the problem.

'What?' I was shocked. 'When? What are you talking about?'

'I guess it was all over before you were even born, but yeah, that's what happened. Mum had an affair with the hairdresser and they split up for a while. So when you were born, Dad wasn't around; they weren't living together.'

'You're kidding.' I was gobsmacked. I never imagined my mother as a woman capable of even getting out of bed on her own, let alone of acting on her physical desires. She had been so helpless my whole life, so I was stunned to learn that she had left my dad for another man for a while. It seemed remarkable. But at the same time, it threw up so many questions.

'What does that mean?' I demanded. 'Am I Dad's daughter? Or is the hairdresser my real dad?'

'Yeah, of course you're Dad's,' Tammy laughed. 'They just went through a rough patch, that's all. And then, when you were born, it wasn't quite sorted out yet so he didn't go along when she registered the birth. And I suppose, because they weren't married, he couldn't go on the certificate automatically.'

She seemed to be treating the whole subject so lightly. I didn't understand why it was all such a big joke to her. My head was in a muddle. This was too much to take in all at once.

'Why didn't they get it sorted out after they got back together then?' I asked. 'I mean, maybe I'm not Dad's daughter. She had an affair.'

'Look, Cassie, you're obviously Dad's because we all look alike, don't we?'

'Do we? I think I look like Mum. I don't look like him. Jesus! Why didn't anyone tell me this before? Why has it taken until now for me to find it out?'

'I don't know,' Tammy said. 'But don't shoot the messenger. It was only an affair, Cassie, it wasn't anything serious.'

Rage suddenly erupted within me. 'Nothing serious! How can you say that? This is my life! These are my parents. Tell me, who is named as the father on *your* birth certificate?'

'Dad.'

'And on Marie's?'

'Dad.'

'But he's not on mine. What does that tell you?'

'Nothing. It just tells you they had split up at the time. They got back together again.'

'I don't know, Tammy. I don't know. Things are starting to make more sense now. I've got to think about this. I've really got to think.'

That night, I didn't get a wink of sleep. My head was so full of memories and recollections. I had always felt like the outsider in the family, but in the past I put that down to the big age gap between me and my sisters. They were a family before I arrived and then, eight years later, I came along. I was like an only child. What if I wasn't really Dad's daughter? Maybe that was why he had always been so hard on me. Maybe that was why he always had a go at me. Perhaps he didn't believe I was really his daughter. It wasn't like he ever showed me an ounce of affection. I'd seen him shower Marie with hugs and kisses and he was easier on Tammy too, though they didn't have an affectionate bond like he had with Marie. But with me, there was nothing. Nothing at all. Why? And maybe that was why he found it so easy to just pick up and leave after my mum died. It wasn't normal, was it, just to leave me to fend for myself after my mother died? I was thirteen. Maybe he didn't feel like he had any responsibility for me. Maybe he wasn't really my dad after all. My parents had never married, so what did that mean? What relationship did we have? If I wasn't his daughter, and he wasn't married to my mum, what did that make us? I didn't know. I needed clarity. I needed some professional advice.

The following morning I called Anna. 'Dad's not on my birth certificate,' I said. 'I've only just found out because it took so long for them to send it down to me. I called up my sister and she told me that Mum had an affair before I was born and they split up briefly. They never got married and he's not named as my father. What does that mean?'

'Erm, I'm not sure.' Anna seemed taken aback.

'I mean, what right has he got to decide what happens to me now? Has he got parental responsibility for me?'

'I don't know. Let me check and get back to you.'

The fact was, I was getting tired of living in foster care. I had been looking after myself all my life and though the stability and kindness shown by Sheila and Adam in the first few months had been welcome, I felt restricted by their house rules. It may have worked fine for their own children but I didn't really feel like a seventeen year old; I felt much older. And being told I had to be home by dinner time each night was irritating. I wanted to live independently. I felt more than ready and, when Jake suggested I move into his mum's place with him, I was keen. I didn't want to be 'looked after' any more or a 'foster child' any more – I wanted to move on with my life.

A meeting was called a week later with representatives of Social Services, my foster parents and myself. Anna explained: 'Technically, Cassie, due to the fact that your birth certificate doesn't actually name your Dad as your father, he doesn't have any parental responsibility for you. Legally, he has no rights with regards to you at all, which means that if you did want to leave foster care now, you would be free to go.'

'Really?'

'Yes, though we would advise you to stay in your current placement till you turn eighteen, as this has obviously been such a positive environment for you.'

'Yes, but Jake's mum is also really nice and Sheila and Adam have met them and they said that they would support the move, isn't that right, Sheila?'

I turned now to my foster mother.

'Yes,' Sheila agreed. 'We see no reason why Cassie can't move in with Jake's family if that's what she wants. Obviously we don't want her to go but if those are her wishes, then we will respect them and support her decision. Cassie is at a crucial period in her life and she is on the cusp of taking the first crucial steps into adulthood and responsibility. If she says she's ready and she wants to go, we'll help her and do everything to help make that transition a success.'

'I see.' Anna nodded. 'Well, what about we leave the placement open for twenty-eight days after the move, just in case things don't go according to plan?'

'Absolutely,' Sheila agreed. 'That sounds like a good back-up plan. Cassie?'

'Yes, that would be great. Thank you. I really am grateful to you and Adam, you know. It's just, well, I feel like I need to have my own life now.'

'It's okay,' said Sheila. 'We understand. You've had independence all your life and I honestly feel you can handle it. Just remember, we're always there for you. You can always come back. Always.'

In October 2012 I moved out of care altogether and into Jake's house with his mum Jeanette, her partner Barry and their younger son Owen. Everyone had to be CRB checked before the move, which was a bit embarrassing, but by then I had confided everything about the police interviews to Jeanette and she was very supportive. They charged us twenty-five pound a week rent and I still saw my foster family once a week. It was lovely living with Jake full time, and while he got up to go out to work every day, I did my job, working to help the police with their major investigation. I loved living with Jake's family – they were very kind people. The family all worked, so if I had a day off from the police interviews, I would enjoy having the place to myself.

While everyone pitched in with the chores, my relationship to Jeanette and Barry was completely different to that with Sheila and Adam. They weren't responsible for me, so I was left to run my own life. The flexibility and freedom meant I could be my own person. I could take decisions about my finances, my future and my day-to-day life. It was nice that I was still able to do this in a homely environment. Often we sat down for dinner together – and I enjoyed making meals for everyone, including Jake's two little boys who often stayed over – but there was no pressure to conform to the family timetable. And that suited me well.

Then, in March 2013, I got a shock when I realised I had missed two periods. At first I hadn't really noticed because I was on the pill and, anyway, my periods had always been fairly erratic. But after I missed the second one, I had a feeling that something wasn't right. On top of that, I had begun to feel queasy first thing in the morning and last thing at night. So, just to be on the safe side, I took a home pregnancy test one evening. The result was not what I was expecting. Pale and shaking, I told Jake I needed to talk to him in private, so we went to his room together.

'I'm pregnant,' I blurted out.

'What? How? You're on the pill, aren't you?'

'Yes. And I'm still taking it. I don't know. It didn't work. I don't know how it happened but I'm pregnant. Look!' I waved the little white wand in front of his face. 'I just did the test. Two lines. Two lines!'

Jake took the wand and stared at it for a while, then he sighed heavily and sat down on the bed, too shocked to say another word. I went to sit next to him. He placed a comforting hand on my knee and I put my hand over his. We stayed like that for a little while and then he pulled me into him in a big bear hug and planted a big kiss on the top of my head.

'It's going to be okay,' he whispered. 'Whatever happens. We'll be fine.'

'I don't want a baby now,' I said tearfully. 'I'm too young. I'm not ready. With everything going on. I mean, how could we have a child?'

'I don't know . . . I just don't know.'

We talked a lot over the next few days. Jake wasn't keen on having a child right then either – after all, he had become a father when he was very young and that relationship hadn't worked out. At first, things had been very messy between him and his ex, and though he was a doting dad, it had taken a long time for them to settle into a routine that suited them both. The friction between them never really went away. And the guilt of not being with his children all the time was a constant sadness in Jake's life. It was understandable that he was scared of rushing into things again.

For my part, I was torn. On the one hand, I knew it was a terrible time to have a baby, given how much time I had to devote to the investigation. On the other hand, I felt haunted by the termination I'd had when I was fifteen. I thought a lot about that now, about what the child I aborted would be like now if I hadn't gone through with it. In my head I knew it was for the best that I hadn't carried that baby to term, but my heart was full of regret and sorrow for the child who'd never had a chance of life. What was the best thing? Neither of us knew. I called my doctor and she made us an appointment at the hospital for a scan.

Jake was there, holding my hand the moment the baby appeared on the screen – a tiny little body, large head and a strong, thumping heart.

'Oh my God,' I breathed, when I saw her for the first time. 'That's our baby!'

Jake gripped my hand tighter but he didn't say a word. The sonographer took the measurements and then gave us the results. The baby was approximately thirteen weeks old. I walked out of there in a daze, clutching the fuzzy pictures, and before I even knew what I was saying the words came tumbling out.

'I want to keep it,' I said. 'I want to keep the baby. Just seeing it and hearing the heartbeat . . . Oh, Jake! I just don't think I can have another termination. I can't go through that again. I can't.' Tears stung my eyes and my throat tightened.

'It's okay. I want to keep it too,' he said, smiling. 'It will be fine. We'll make it work.'

I was so relieved I threw myself into Jake's arms. I had always wanted to be a mother, and after the termination I worried I would never get another chance. The guilt had worried at me intensely, making me fearful for the future. What if that was it? What if I never got pregnant again? On top of all of that, there was something else in the back of my mind – my mum. Huntington's was hereditary. There was a fifty per cent chance that I had inherited it from my mum, in which case I knew I had to have my children early. I had always envied my sisters for the good times they had shared with our mother – the memories they had of her being well and happy and caring for them the way a normal mother does. By the time I was old enough to start school, she was an invalid. If I had children, I didn't want them to know me in that way.

So we shared the news with Jeanette and Barry, Sheila and Adam and Anna, and everyone was very supportive. The sickness passed quickly and then the heartburn kicked in, but the physical symptoms didn't bother me too much. The hardest part was carrying on with the investigation while I was pregnant. In May that year the police started making their arrests, and every time they went after somebody I was gripped by fear and panic. As part of this process I was required to do video identifications on an almost daily basis and this, too, was painful. Just seeing their faces again was harrowing, bringing up awful memories that I'd long tried to forget. I felt the baby moving inside me and the recollections of what they did to me hurt more than it had ever done before. *How could they? How could they have abused a child like that?*

Mina shared with me some of the statements that the men made. Several admitted to having sex with me but they said I had lied about my age so they thought it was consensual. One of them said I had served him while I was working in a club and then I had gone home with him, which was strange because I'd never worked in a club in my life. Many refused to comment and then called in their lawyers. More evidence was discovered – Mina said they had recovered the footage on Maj's phone of the night they had first taken me to a hotel: they had the video of one of the men putting his cock in my mouth. I was shocked – I never imagined the footage would still exist after all this time and I felt a mixture of shame, embarrassment and horror at the thought of all the police officers watching the footage. But at the same time, I was pleased. I was pleased that the evidence was there. The most extraordinary thing was that Akim, my old neighbour, actually handed himself in! I never expected that. He came forward and admitted what he had done. He was the only one.

Phones were seized, computers, cars, all sorts of things. And Mina was good at keeping me up to date – she said that the phone evidence proved that the men were in touch with one another, and knew one another. Further arrests were made – family men, men who were never suspected of doing anything illegal. There was a lot of upset within the Pakistani communities where the majority of the arrests were being made, but the police were ready for this. They said they were keen to work with communities to tackle the issues surrounding the alleged crimes.

'It's the biggest investigation we've ever had of this kind,' Mina explained. 'We've arrested fifty-four suspects as a result of your evidence. Clearly there is a problem here. Evidently something has gone wrong. Our main focus, of course, is to bring the criminals to justice, but beyond that we have to work with the communities to see that nothing like this is allowed to happen again.'

Over the summer, just after I turned eighteen, I had another test – the test for the Huntington's gene. It was the first opportunity I'd had to be tested and I was six months' pregnant at the time.

By now I had found out that we were expecting a little girl and I was thrilled – I had always wanted a daughter – but I also needed to know what sort of future I could expect to enjoy. Would I be healthy? Would I be around to look after my little girl? I needed to know the truth. Two weeks after the test, Jake and I returned to the hospital and they showed us into a little room where we were handed the results in an envelope. I opened it and a small sigh escaped my lips, like air escaping from a balloon. It was positive. I had the gene. I handed the piece of paper to Jake, and when he read the results he threw his arms around me and squeezed me tight. I looked at him sadly. I felt like I'd known all along; it went through all the girls in our family. Now it was confirmed. I didn't cry. I just nodded and asked the doctor, 'What do I do now?'

'If you get any symptoms, contact your GP. You probably know quite a lot about the symptoms and signs because of your mum, but we have some leaflets here for you to take away. As you know, it can be triggered at any time and at any age, so don't assume, just because you're young, that it won't happen. The disease is unpredictable that way. Once we see the first signs, there's usually a deterioration over about a fifteen-year period.'

Jake tried his best to be upbeat on the way home; he told me he would be there for me and take care of me, no matter what, but I was numb, lost in my thoughts. He was so kind, so well-meaning, but he really had no idea what to expect of this disease. He didn't know how disabled I would eventually become. The day-to-day struggle of trying to love someone who is so utterly dependent would test the strongest of relationships. I had seen it with my own family. I had been there, trying to pick up the pieces when my family broke apart. And if me and Jake were to split up, then what? What would happen to me? Who would take care of me?

For the next few weeks I carried the weight of the world on my shoulders. My future was so bleak I couldn't bear to think about it. It brought back all the memories of caring for my mum, recalling how disabled she had been, how restricted she had been. What sort of a life did she have? By the end, she was nothing – not a person at all but a mass of symptoms. It was worse than a death sentence – knowing that the end would be long, drawn- out and traumatic for all my loved ones. It felt so unfair. The worst part was knowing that I was expecting a little girl; knowing I had a fifty per cent chance of passing it on to her too. What sort of life would she have? Would she grow up wiping her mum's bottom, knowing this was in store for her too? What was I bringing her into this world for? For a lifetime of suffering?

For a while the news took me to some dark places. I was overwhelmed with guilt and sorrow – and fear. Terrible fear of the person I would eventually become. Some days it was hard just to get out of bed; those were the days I didn't know why I should bother. It took some weeks, but gradually the clouds began to clear.

The fact was, I didn't have time to get depressed, as life got in the way. I had a baby growing inside me, interviews to do, a life to lead. I could sit around all day feeling sorry for myself or I could get on with living my life the best way possible. What good would it do to worry about the future? I couldn't change it so there was no point fretting. I had to live for the now. I had to try and enjoy the time I did have while I was well. Seven weeks before the birth, Jake and I got our own council house. It had taken a lot of time and patience, but we were finally successful in bidding on a property. We moved into a lovely two-bedroom house in the countryside, about ten miles outside of town.

Jeanette was amazing. She helped us move and decorate the place while a Moving House Grant from Social Services allowed us to buy the essentials like a fridge-freezer, cooker, curtains and carpets. Right up until my due date in October we were getting the house sorted out, and we were just about ready with the cot and the baby's room, then my due date came and went, and nothing happened. It was frustrating but I tried to keep myself busy around the house. Two days went by, then three, and I started to feel panicky. The doctors let me go seven days overdue before they said they would have to induce me.

I thought I was more than ready to give birth but I wasn't prepared for the pain after the induction, so I had to get an epidural. After thirteen long hours, I started to feel frightened. I was tired, I found it hard to push and it looked like the baby was getting distressed. Jeanette and Jake were by my side the whole time, encouraging me to keep going, but I was so exhausted I wanted to give up. The doctors came and went. I felt helpless and out of control. It was horrible. At one point they started talking about a C-section but, in the final few minutes, I managed to bear down really hard while the midwife got hold of my baby with the forceps and she came out in one last push.

Panting and exhausted, I lay back waiting for the cry. I held my breath and gripped Jake's hand, looking anxiously at the nurses for a sign that all was well. When I finally heard my daughter's hiccuppy little wail for the first time, I was so overcome with relief I broke down in tears. The midwife cleaned her up, did the fingers and toes test and then handed her to me. My little girl. From the moment I set eyes on her, I was entranced. The forceps had squashed her little head into a strange cone-shape but I didn't care. In truth, I didn't even notice. To me, she was just gorgeous. Just 5 lbs 10 ounces, she was tiny, but every inch of her was perfect. We named her Elsa.

Motherhood came easily to me. I don't know why but it felt so right and so natural, the love just came pouring out. It helped that Elsa was an easy baby. She didn't cry much, she didn't get sick and she took to the breast very easily. She was just perfect. Of course, the arrests were all still going on so that made me feel extra protective towards her.

One morning, when Elsa was about two months old, I was called by the police with news of three more arrests. Later that day I spotted an Asian man sat outside the house in a car, not going anywhere. He seemed to be watching my house. I felt jumpy and paranoid so I pressed the police alarm that had been fitted in the house before we moved in. By the time the police arrived, the man had gone but I still felt frightened and insecure for the next few days.

My family all came to visit within Elsa's first year – Dad, Tammy, Marie and Dara – and it was so nice to see them all again, and to introduce them to Jake and our new baby girl. I was proud of the way I had managed to start my life again and I hoped they would be pleased for me too. But something felt strange; there was a distance between us now that was more than simple geography. I struggled to make a connection with my dad after such a long time apart. I told him about the police case and he said he was sorry about what happened to me, but he didn't apologise for the way he had treated me and I didn't feel ready to confront him about his violence. Or indeed, to ask him about my paternity. I was just too scared of what I might find out. Still, it was lovely to be reunited with them all, if only for a short time. And for the first year after Elsa's birth, everything was fine. The investigation went on, Jake was working, I was looking after the baby. But then, in 2014, Jake had a breakdown.

It happened so suddenly, and seemed to come completely out of the blue. One morning he was at work and then, in an instant, he was overcome with fear. He couldn't do it. He couldn't cope. He left that day and never went back. For a couple of months he just sat at home, convinced that he would wake up the next morning and everything would be fine again, but this never happened and eventually I managed to convince him to see the doctor. He was referred for counselling. In the meantime, we were living on the breadline. Without Jake's regular income we were on benefits and they barely covered the basics. Within six months we were visiting the food bank every week. Jeanette and Sheila helped out as much as they could but we were living a hand-to-mouth existence, only just able to afford the gas and electricity bills. And the police work rolled on. I was still being interviewed regularly, picked up by to do drive rounds, interviews, video identifications. When I was driven up to Halifax, I had to stay overnight in a hotel and I hated that. I had come to really hate being in hotels – they were so soulless and impersonal and, of course, they reminded me of the nights I had been taken there by the men. I had been offered counselling myself for the panic attacks and the nightmares but I didn't feel ready to go through that.

At least now I had Elsa along with me, and looking after her made all the difference. Elsa made me happy in a way nothing else could. With the counselling and lots of support from our families, Jake slowly recovered and went back to work. And still the investigation rolled on . . . There were times I thought it would never end and it was incredibly disheartening when the police had to let off some suspects, either from lack of evidence or because they did deals to inform on others.

Finally, in February 2015, twenty-five men were charged for committing fifty-eight offences against me including rape, sexual activity with a child under sixteen and trafficking. During the course of the investigation one girl had also come forward and was due to give evidence for another offence. The rest of the crimes were all related to me. The men were named in the local Halifax paper and I showed a copy to Jake online. Until that moment, I don't think he had imagined the scale of the investigation. Now it was there in black and white.

'It seems like a lot,' he said under his breath, going through the list.

'It's not enough,' I said. 'I wanted them all charged.'

But for Halifax, at least, it was big deal: the largest CSE investigation in the country, bigger even than Rochdale and Rotherham. By the time the court dates came around in May 2016 the whole case had been going on for four years – 5,900 lines of enquiry had been pursued, 733 interviews had been conducted, 1754 statements taken, 2812 exhibits seized, 90 premises and 21 vehicles searched, 413 phones and sim cards taken and 156 computers. And I was pregnant with my second child.

But after four long years I was ready. I was ready for justice, ready to give my evidence and ready to get my life back.

18.

The Trials

LOOKING IN THE BATHROOM mirror, I applied my eyeliner with a steady hand. Then I swept my eyelashes with black mascara and carefully applied sheer lip-gloss. Elsa toddled into the bathroom holding up her favourite soft teddy.

'Teddy, Mummy! It's Teddy!' She pushed the soft toy into my legs and I took it from her, smiling fondly.

'It is Teddy, isn't it?' I bent down and examined the dog-eared floppy soft toy. I had bought it for her when she was just a little baby and she'd hardly slept a night without it, though now it was worn down and the fluffy tufts in the ears were almost entirely gone. Of course that didn't matter to Elsa. Teddy came with us on all our trips away from home. I dreaded to think about how I'd get her to sleep without it.

'Sorry!' Jake called through from the bedroom. He appeared in the doorway now and gave our daughter a mock-cross look.

'There you are, madam!' he exclaimed. 'I told you not to

disturb Mummy while she's getting ready. Come on, let's finish your hair.'

He took her little hand in his and explained: 'She escaped me while I was trying to brush her hair. You look nice. You okay?'

I nodded. 'Yeah, I'm fine.'

It was May 2016 and the first day of the trials. We were staying in a hotel in Liverpool close to the courtroom where I was going to be interviewed. The trials themselves were taking place in Leeds but my evidence was going to be given via video link. I had been well prepared by the police and social workers on what to expect and, after four long years giving statements and interviews, I was pleased that it was all finally coming to a head. Over the next three days I would be giving evidence against twenty-four men in three separate trials, which meant eight barristers would be cross-examining me at each trial. Out of all the men who had been charged, only my neighbour Akim pleaded guilty.

Elsa was often up at the crack of dawn but I'd beaten her to it this morning, my eyes pinging open at 5 a.m. It was almost a relief to hear her shifting about in her cot – looking after Elsa was a welcome distraction from the thought of what lay ahead of me. I busied myself sorting out her porridge and milk, trying not to think about the rest of the day. But when Jake asked if I wanted to go down to breakfast with him, I couldn't face it. I had no appetite. After putting on my black leggings, burgundy blouse and black ankle boots, I went into the bathroom to put on my make-up and tie my long brown hair back in a ponytail.

Gazing at my reflection in the bathroom mirror, I marvelled at how much older I was than when all this started eight years earlier. I was a twelve-year-old child when those men started abusing me. I was twenty now and a mother myself. Having a daughter of my own brought it all home to me, how those men had picked on a vulnerable and innocent young girl in need of friendship and affection for their own sick lusts. But those men weren't facing a child now, they were facing an adult – a woman who had been to hell and back and was strong enough to face them again for one reason and for one reason only: to make them pay for their crimes.

I was angry, furious even, that of all the men who had been charged only Akim had admitted what he had done. The rest were fighting the charges, which meant I had to give evidence. As if it wasn't enough what they had done to me! On top of that, they were putting me through the ordeal of a trial. I guess they all hoped I would fall at the final hurdle, but I'd been through too much, sacrificed too much to let them beat me. Twenty-four barristers all throwing questions at me? Let them do their worst. I took one last look in the mirror and pulled my ponytail tight. *Let's do it!*

'Okay? Ready?' Jake asked as I walked back into the bedroom of the hotel. He had Elsa's carrier all ready to go. I nodded and together we eased Elsa into the backpack, fastened the shoulder straps and then Jake hoisted her onto his back and I grabbed her toy bag, filled to bursting with books, stuffed animals, plastic toys, as well as her sippy cup, spoon and a million snacks. Jake's job was to keep our daughter occupied for the whole day while I was giving evidence, so we had come well prepared.

'Okay, looks like we're all ready,' I said, and the three of us left the hotel room and went down to reception where my social worker Anna was waiting for us. She gave me a reassuring hug and asked me how I was feeling.

'Good,' I replied. She seemed more anxious than I did, so I went on: 'Elsa slept through last night so I got a good night's sleep. I feel fine. Honestly.'

'Did you eat?'

I shook my head. 'I'm not hungry.'

Together we walked five minutes down the street to the Crown Court and I was shown into the special room where I was to give my evidence.

'Kiss bye bye!' I turned to Elsa and gave her a big kiss and a hug.

'Have fun with Daddy! Be a good girl.'

'Bye bye, Mummy. Kith kith,' she lisped back and landed two sloppy kisses on both cheeks, holding my face firmly with her tiny hands. Jake gave me a big hug and whispered: 'You can do it. Good luck!'

Then it was time.

I was shown into the room where a plump middle-aged lady in a black jacket introduced herself as Jean, the Witness Assistant. She said that she was there to help me, and if there was anything I needed, to just ask her. There was a camera trained on me and a large screen opposite which showed a live video link to the courtroom in Leeds. I could see the courtroom now and they could also see me. I had been offered a screen to hide my face but I'd refused – no, I wanted the jury to see me. I wanted them to see my face and know that I was telling the truth. The judge was already seated when they turned my camera on, as well as all the defendants and their barristers. My heart started to thump in my chest. This was one of the scariest things I'd ever done. *Stay strong, Cassie. You can do this.*

The judge introduced himself as Judge Geoffrey Marson. He welcomed me and then Jean helped me swear the oath on the Bible. I did as I was instructed, standing up and taking hold of the book. Then I read the words on the little card Jean handed me: 'I swear by Almighty God that I will tell the truth, the whole truth and nothing but the truth.'

And it was funny, but just hearing my own voice say those words gave me courage. The thing was I did have the truth on my side. They may have had expensive lawyers with their posh voices and silly wigs, but all those men were lying. I had nothing to fear because all I had to do was tell the truth. The CPS had also given me some guidance about speaking in court and I now tried to recall what they said as I waited for the questions to start: speak slowly, don't get confused, answer all the questions, don't get angry and don't swear!

Judge Marson explained that first the prosecuting barrister for the Crown Prosecution Service (CPS) Michelle Colborne QC would take me through my evidence against the defendants, and then the defence barristers, all eight, would have the chance to question me. He seemed very kind and said that I should feel free at any point to speak up if I needed a break or didn't understand a question. So the first part was fairly straightforward – the barrister representing the CPS got up and helped me give me evidence against all these men and then, one by one, the defence barristers rose to their feet, introduced themselves and started firing questions at me. I tried my best but initially it was a bit confusing.

'I'm sorry, I don't know who you are talking about,' I said fairly early on.

'Mr Hedar Ali,' the barrister repeated himself. 'This gentleman here – the one you say picked you up from the middle of the Yorkshire Dales.' His tone was sceptical, disbelieving.

'Oh, Tupac!' I said. 'I'm sorry, but your client didn't give me his real name. None of them told me their names, so I didn't know him as Mr Hedar Ali – but yes, he did pick me up from the moors. And I saw him several times after that.'

Once I got going I was fine answering the questions. I spoke loudly and clearly and, though I was angry, I was careful to maintain my composure. It was hard. The lies these men were telling was enough to make my blood boil. Tupac had even written to me from prison and his love letters were read out in court. Several of the barristers put it to me that I had told their clients I was over sixteen and therefore I had entrapped them.

'But he knew how old I was,' I responded to one. 'He picked me up from school loads of times, and I was always in my school uniform. I never hid my age. I never lied about it. If anyone asked me I told them the truth. I had no reason to lie.'

The questions came thick and fast. One of the barristers claimed I was working in a bar when I'd met their client, and that I'd said I was nineteen on the night I supposedly served him. Then, apparently, I had gone back to his house and we'd had legal, consensual sex. I was amazed that this fantastical story had been presented to the court.

'How could I be working in a bar when I was at school and had no fake ID?' I countered. 'I've never owned any fake ID. I've never worked in a bar in my life. It's just a load of lies.'

The worst part was when the barristers repeated the same questions in different ways, as if trying to catch me out.

'And you say that you were taken to a hotel that night – can you be sure my client was there at all? You do admit to having taken a fair amount of drink and drugs that night.'

'Yes, it's him. I recognise him. I picked him out in a video identification parade of nine people.'

'How can you be sure? We're talking about a time nearly five years ago. You were drunk and on drugs at the time.'

'I remember him,' I repeated.

'You say you don't know his name. Are you sure this is the same man?'

'I didn't know any of their real names,' I said. 'None of them told me their real names but I know it's him because I recognise him. I don't know how else to say it to you – I recognise him. He raped me – I remember his face.'

'Is there a small possibility at all that you could be wrong? Let's look at this objectively – you were on drugs, you were drunk, you were young, it was night time and my client is a respected and upstanding member of his community, a family man who has never been in trouble with the law before in his life. Do you allow for the possibility, however small, that you might actually be mistaken?'

'No, I've told you. It was him.'

It was very frustrating to be accused of lying or 'entrapping' these men but I kept my cool throughout. Even when the camera was flying from one barrister to the next, trying to keep up with all the different questions, I did my best to answer them all calmly. In the end it was Jean who lost her temper.

'Your Honour, this is really quite a pace for the young woman,' Jean cut in as I struggled with the latest round of questions. 'I do think the learned friends need to be a little bit patient and take care not to put the witness under too much pressure. Perhaps they could slow down with their questioning?'

'Yes, quite right,' the judge agreed. 'If we could proceed at a slower pace for the witness, that would be preferable. Learned friends, do remember to give the witness time to consider her response before asking your next question. I agree with and thank the Witness Assistant for her contribution.'

I was pleased that Jean had interrupted; it was all becoming a bit much for me. When the judge said that it was time for lunch, she showed me out of the video room and then put a comforting hand on my shoulder.

'All you alright, pet?' she asked, sympathetically. 'Them barristers were going at it like the clappers! I hope the judge gets them to slow down this afternoon.'

'I'm alright, thanks,' I said, suddenly ravenous. She showed me into the waiting room where Jake was sitting on the floor, doing a jigsaw puzzle with Elsa.

'Hi! How did it go?'

'Okay,' I said. 'Have you got something for me to eat? I'm starving.'

The three of us ate some sandwiches together and I played with Elsa for a little bit before I was called back into the witness room at 2 p.m. The afternoon was almost as bad as the morning, and I noted Jean tutting a couple of times when the barristers were overloading me with questions. I did my best. It was all I could do. Finally, at 4 p.m., the judge said that the cross-examinations were over and thanked me for giving my evidence. I'd been in the witness box for six hours.

That evening, at the hotel, I couldn't say much to Jake at first. I was so exhausted I could barely speak. But later, lying on the bed, I hugged Elsa before allowing myself to shed a few tears.

'It's the way they spoke to me,' I explained to Jake. 'Like I'm just a young, stupid kid who has taken too many drugs and can't remember what's happened to me. It's the way they were implying that I was just a waste of time and these were really important family men who had never done anything wrong all their lives. Like I was the troublemaker! It just felt unfair. Really unfair. Really wrong.'

'It's only two more days and then it'll all be over,' he reasoned. 'Then you won't have to think about this at all. You can just get on with your life.' He reached out to stroke my hair but I pulled away.

'Don't,' I said gently. 'You know I don't like that.'

'I'm sorry,' he sighed. 'I'm sorry. I forgot.'

It was one of my hang-ups, one of the things that reminded me of the rapes: I couldn't bear anyone touching my face, neck or head. And I hated anyone stroking my hair.

'I'm giving it everything I have,' I said determinedly. 'I'm not going to let them beat me. At least I know what to expect for tomorrow.'

At that moment Elsa appeared at my feet holding up her favourite bath toy – a squidgy blue plastic whale that squirted water out of its blowhole. Jake and I both laughed.

'I think Elsa's trying to tell us something,' he said.

'Yeah.' I grinned indulgently. 'I'll do bath time tonight. You've had her all day. I think she needs some Mummy time.'

The next day I was up at 6 a.m. and, although I was still nervous, I felt a little more prepared than I had the previous day. At least I now knew what to expect. On day two, when the questioning became a little aggressive, instead of waiting for Jean to step in, I asked the judge if the barristers could please slow down their questions. Again the barristers attacked me and questioned my ability to remember their clients, given the circumstances, but I held my nerve and repeated in a calm, steady voice that I was quite sure it was them. *Breathe. Stay focused,* I told myself. I refused to be beaten down or thrown off course. There was too much at stake, too much riding on my evidence. For the most part I was the only witness in these cases. I understand Sam gave evidence against one man, Talib, but for the rest of them, it was just me.

Occasionally the camera panned across the jury and I got a little look at the faces of the people who were judging the trials. Judging me. I tried not to think too much about them but I did wonder: can they see the truth? Do they believe me? I hoped so. At the end of the third day, the judge thanked me for my evidence and I was let out of the witness room. Jean gave my shoulder a squeeze and her eyes crinkled in a broad smile. 'Well done,' she whispered. I walked out, slowly, steadily, feeling triumphant. *Whatever happens now, I've done my bit.* I was drained and emotionally battered but I also felt a huge sense of accomplishment.

From the first faltering conversations with Pete, through all the years of hard work in getting to this point, it had been an incredibly long and difficult journey. There were so many times I felt like giving up, so many times I heard the phone ringing and didn't want to pick it up because I knew it would be the police with more demands and questions. There were times when I wanted to just forget it all. But I didn't give in. Jake kept encouraging me, helping me, giving me motivation when I was at my lowest ebb. Now he stood at the end of the corridor, his arms wide open, eyes shining with pride.

'I did it,' I whispered to him, as I fell into his embrace.

'You did it,' he agreed.

'I bet they thought I wouldn't manage it. I reckon they thought I wouldn't make it. Well, I showed them. I hope they all go down.'

'I'm so proud of you,' Jake said, smothering me in a massive bear hug.

Anna was in tears as she greeted me. Apart from Jake, she was the only other person who had been there to support me throughout the trials. My dad and sisters were told about the court cases – they knew how serious this was and yet not one of them had turned up to show me moral support. They were even offered lifts by Social Services to get to the trials but they didn't take them up. They didn't bother to call or text on the days I gave my evidence. It felt like a real kick in the teeth and I must admit that, after that, I lost the desire to keep up with regular telephone contact. Why should I bother? Having been through the trauma of the abuse in the first place, and then finding the courage to go through with the trials, I felt let down that neither my father nor my sisters had been there when I needed them most. In contrast, Anna had been there throughout, offering help and encouragement in my darkest moments. She was the family I never had, the person who was always there, no matter what. Together, we had been on this journey.

'Whatever happens now, Cassie, you should feel really proud of yourself. You did brilliantly,' she said.

What will happen now? I wondered.

19.

The Verdicts

IT WAS A LOVELY sunny afternoon in May, just a few days after I finished giving my evidence in Leeds, and I was in Jake's mum's garden with Elsa. By my feet lay a steaming mug of tea, while in my hand I held a little tube of bubble mixture. I took the small plastic wand, pursed my lips and blew a steady stream of bubbles for Elsa, who shrieked with delight and chased after the dancing globes, through the lawn and pink-flecked flowerbeds. I watched with wonder as she ran about in the sunshine, pale-yellow dress billowing, her arms extended upwards, laughing as the bubbles drifted higher and higher into the sky. She was such a happy little girl, I thought. She lived entirely in the moment. Together, in the sunshine, we could spend hours lost in our own little world, a world of rainbow bubbles, joy and laughter. Once the cloud of bubbles had drifted beyond her reach, she ran back to me in the middle of the garden and demanded 'more, more, more'. I picked up the wand again and dipped it into the mix, ready to unleash another burst of bubbles into the air. It was a delightful game and a relief from the days of being on the witness stand. But as soon as the phone rang, I knew what it was about and I was almost too scared to answer. Tentatively, I lifted the phone to my ear.

'Cassie? It's Pete here. I've got the verdicts.' His voice gave nothing away. My heart began to pound. I had to swallow hard. Beyond the flowerbeds I watched Elsa dance up towards the patio on her tiptoes, trying to catch a giant bubble that was floating just beyond her reach.

Just breathe, I told myself. *Relax. Breathe.*

'Okay,' I said slowly. 'What's the result?'

'It's good news, Cassie. No. It's *great* news. You did it! I've got the verdicts in from the first trial and, well, I'll read you the results. You ready?'

'Yes.'

'Okay, here goes: Hedar Ali, thirty-six, of Bradford, has been found guilty of two counts of rape and two counts of trafficking for sexual exploitation. Haidar Ali, forty-one, of Halifax: guilty of sexual activity with a child and causing a person to engage in sexual activity with a child. Mohammad Ramzan, thirty-five, of Bradford: guilty of rape. Haaris Ahmed, thirty-two, of Halifax: guilty of two counts of sexual activity with a child and supply of class B drugs. Taukeer Butt, thirty-one, of Halifax: guilty of four counts of sexual activity with a child and Amaar Ali Ditta, twenty-seven, from Halifax: guilty of two counts of sexual activity with a child. Guilty, guilty, guilty! You did it, Cassie. You did it! They'll all be sentenced at a later date. But, Cassie, that's all of them from the first trial. All of them! Cassie . . . are you there? Cassie?'

I couldn't speak. The tears were streaming down my cheeks.

It felt like I'd been holding my breath for four long years and now finally, *finally* I could stop. My hand flew to my mouth and great wracking sobs welled up from somewhere deep inside me. Silently, my whole body shook.

'Cassie? Cassie? Are you there? Are you okay?'

The jury had believed me. They were all going to prison.

I let out a massive sigh. 'Yes, I'm here,' I sniffed, swiping at my wet face. 'I'm here. I'm just . . . I can't believe it. Thank you, Pete. Thank you. For everything.' I hung up and tried to compose myself but it was no good, I just couldn't stop the tears. It was like a dam had broken inside me and all the emotion of the last four years came pouring out. Sitting there outside in the sunshine, I cried my heart out, weeping into my hands.

'Mummy?' Elsa tugged at my sleeve. 'Mummy?'

'I'm okay, darling.' I scooped her up into my lap and cuddled her, burying my head in her soft blonde curls. 'They're not sad tears, they're happy tears, darling. Mummy's really happy.'

The following day I got the results of the second trial and, a day later, just after I dropped Elsa at nursery, the third trial results came in. In total seventeen of the defendants had been found guilty of the crimes they committed against me, while seven had either been found not guilty or cleared on direction of the judge. The police were delighted with the results and I was happy too. I felt that I had done my bit to make Halifax a safer place for young girls. And yet . . . and yet . . .

'Are you pleased?' Jake asked me that night as I lay in bed, staring up at the ceiling.

'I am, yes,' I said hesitantly.

'But?'

'But, well, I wanted to get them all, Jake. I wanted them to get rid of them all. I mean, including my old neighbour, who pleaded guilty, that's only eighteen.'

'Only? Eighteen doesn't sound like a small number to me,' he said, frowning.

'Yeah, but they found a hundred numbers on my phone. They had arrested fifty-four originally, and to think only eighteen out of all those men have been convicted – it just means they're all still out there. All those other ones, they got away with it.'

Jake was silent for a moment: 'Well, they could only prosecute the ones where they felt there was a reasonable chance of conviction. They just couldn't prove it. That's what the police told you.'

'I know.'

'So what do you want to do about it?'

'I don't know,' I said, biting my thumb. 'Nothing, I suppose. What else *can* I do?'

A couple of weeks later the men were sentenced – and I was pleased to hear that many had gone down for long periods. In total the men got 168 years prison time between them. Hedar Ali, or Tupac as I knew him, got twenty-five years; Haaris Ahmed, Harry, was sent down for twelve and a half years for two counts of sexual activity with a child and supplying Class B drugs. My neighbour, who I knew as Akim, was sentenced to six years jail time after pleading guilty to two counts of sexual activity with a child. It was pleasing to know that some of the men who had abused me were going to lose their freedom for a very long time. I had already lost so much of my life to them that I felt it was no less than they deserved.

In June, the story came out in the press, and for the first time I learned that this had been the largest and longest-running investigation into CSE in the UK. For a few weeks after the trials ended, the details of the cases weren't released because there were other ongoing trials and the police were concerned the results could prejudice the outcomes. But now all the trials were over. Neither Sam nor I were named in the reports. It had been explained to me fairly early on that the law protects the identity of anyone who is a victim of a sexual crime. Peter Mann, Head of the Complex Casework Unit, CPS Yorkshire and Humberside, told the press:

'We have worked closely with our colleagues at West Yorkshire Police since the start of this complex and lengthy operation. These men are responsible for a range of crimes involving Child Sexual Exploitation and abuse. Both these young women have shown immense courage and bravery in reporting these matters to the police and in providing evidence to enable us to bring a strong prosecution case to put before a jury.

'This case sends out a very clear message to all those who may be hesitating about coming forward to report matters such as these. Make no mistake – we will not tolerate this type of abuse on our streets or in our communities. We will not hesitate to bring dangerous criminals who carry out acts of sexual violence to justice.'

Now I got to read what the judge said about the men who

abused me. It had been a strange experience, being the chief prosecution witness for all these trials. While undoubtedly the crimes had been committed against me, in the end I was just there to give evidence. I hadn't been there during some of the crucial moments. Jailing the four convicted of the most serious offences, Judge Geoffrey Marson QC, said about me: 'She was given alcohol, drugs and money for sex. There was no love, no affection, no care. She was taken advantage of when she was drunk and under the influence of drugs.

'She was subjected to humiliation and degradation at the hands of men who used and abused her for their own sexual gratification. It must have been obvious to anyone who came into contact with her that she was particularly vulnerable.'

He went on: 'She was sometimes in such a state of intoxication she was incapable of consenting to any form of sexual activity and that would have been obvious to anyone in her company.

'She has been removed away from home and family on a permanent basis. Psychological damage in this case is about as bad as it gets. She will carry this abuse with her for the rest of her life.'

He said they were not my only abusers but each man bore some responsibility for the damage inflicted. And he added: 'Not one of you has shown the slightest remorse for what you did.'

By now, of course, I knew I was pregnant again, and though this pregnancy wasn't planned either, I was pleased to be having a little brother or sister for Elsa. The threat of Huntington's hung over my whole life, and though I tried not to think about it too much, it was always there, lurking in the back of my mind.

244

If I wanted a family, I had no time to waste. If I wanted my children to grow up with a mother capable of caring for them, I had better have them now. And one thing I was sure of, I didn't want Elsa to be an only child. So Jake and I agreed to have the baby and I enjoyed being pregnant again. The morning sickness passed fairly quickly and it was a relief not to have the pressure of the police work and trials hanging over me. The cases were over. In many ways I was freer than I had been in a very long time, though certain restrictions were still very much present in my day-to-day life.

I was under police protection for my own safety. So where other people took it for granted that they could see their family any time, I never went back to Halifax to see them, and they didn't know where I lived either. I had already experienced one scare where the police had to move me to a different area, and they thought it would be safer if I didn't reveal the location of my home to anyone up in Halifax. So I didn't go on social media, I didn't talk to my family much, and, when I did, I had to use an untraceable mobile phone. I never went on holiday, I had no education – so I couldn't get a job – and I didn't have many friends because it was just too hard to think about trying to explain my background to somebody I'd just met. How could I be normal? How could I share my past with anybody?

I walked around town and felt different from everyone else. The trials were over, it was true, and, as everyone said, I could just 'get on' with my life, but my life was now permanently disrupted by my experiences. And limited too. The judge said I had suffered serious psychological damage and that was true – I still had panic attacks and was frightened of going out on my own.

As soon as the trials were over the council ordered a Serious Case Review into my case, to analyse what had happened to me and how it could be prevented from happening again in the future. I spoke to the author, Barry Raynes, and he collected all the relevant Social Services and police files. Then, when his report came out in October of 2016, I was shocked to learn how many times it had been flagged up that I was potentially a victim of CSE and nobody had said a word to me. Barry's report described in painstaking detail how many social workers had had contact with me – eight, in the years I was in Halifax – and yet, despite numerous attempts by the school, youth workers and the police, I had been failed by the authorities.

In the report, in which I was named 'Jeanette', I could see for the first time that even when certain individuals identified me as a victim of CSE, there was a real lack of effort and interest from managers to do something to help. Pete himself came up against problems: he actively stopped the police from prosecuting me for possession of the Class A drug in April 2011, arguing with his managers that it was wrong to treat me as a criminal. In fact, it was thanks to him that the police sent a strong email at this time, calling on Social Services to convene a child protection conference around me. More than anyone, I saw how important his efforts had been in rescuing me from my situation. I felt such overwhelming gratitude to him at this point. I read in the papers that Richard Burrows, independent chair of the Safeguarding Children Board, said: 'Three main agencies, Calderdale Council's

Children's Social Care team, the NHS and West Yorkshire Police, initially failed to protect Jeanette, despite attempts made by some very committed individual professionals.'

Detective Superintendent Darren Minton, of West Yorkshire Police's Safeguarding Central Governance Unit said the force accepted the findings in the review and admitted there were missed opportunities.

'We would firstly like to apologise to the victim for the failings of West Yorkshire police. We would also like to thank her for her immense courage and bravery in making the disclosures, and giving her evidence which led to the convictions of seventeen men for the sexual offences against her. We hope that the lengthy sentences they received have allowed her to move on from what has undoubtedly been a distressing time in her life. West Yorkshire Police accepts that opportunities were missed in the past to protect victims of Child Sexual Exploitation. It is important to stress that it is a top priority and we now have strong partnerships and better working practices with agencies. The signs of Child Sexual Exploitation are now identified and acted on at an early stage and measures are put in place to protect victims of the abhorrent crime. This improved understanding has also led to a number of cases across West Yorkshire, where perpetrators have been given lengthy jail sentences for sexual offences, some committed decades ago. There is no time limit on justice. We want victims to feel confident and be reassured that they will be taken seriously, treated sensitively and that we will investigate every report thoroughly.'

After reading the report, I contacted Irwin Mitchell Solicitors, who advised me that I had a case against Calderdale Metropolitan Borough Council for failing in their duty of care towards me. I wanted answers. I wanted to know why and how this had happened to me. Over the next few months we uncovered some interesting facts. We found out that social workers knew, when I was just a year old, that my father was physically abusive, that he abused drugs and alcohol and went missing for days at a time. Social Services also knew that my mother was ill, and that the bulk of the caring work fell to me and my sisters. Yet it was puzzling that we had never been identified as young carers, and so we were not offered any support. Through my Social Services files, I learned that as early as June 2009 a youth worker flagged up a concern that I was a victim of CSE and noted too that my father was violent towards me – and yet nothing was done!

In August the same year the police found me in a house with two Asian men and also flagged up concerns about CSE but, once again, nothing was done. I shook my head as I read these words. I just couldn't understand why nobody did anything. It was maddening. If somebody had acted on this information in 2009 I could have been spared two years of the worst kind of abuse anyone can imagine. In the files there was also mention of my father's 'physically and emotionally abusive and neglectful parenting'. The social workers knew! They knew he beat me. As early as April 2010 he even admitted that he hit me to the social workers, and yet, once again, nobody did anything about it. Those men might have preyed on me like vultures, but if it wasn't for my dad I would never have been out there in the first place.

In February 2010 Social Services received the third CSE referral and, yet again, in March, a family support worker flagged it up. But nothing was done to progress child protection investigations. Again and again, the information was there, people tried to bring it to the attention of the authorities. And yet, nothing was done. The social workers came and went, some lasting only a few days or weeks, and most of them I couldn't remember. It was just a sea of unremarkable faces and unmemorable encounters. I had no bond, no connection to any of them, and I knew they would probably be gone in a week's time anyway, so what was the point in talking to them? I told them I'd been out, chilling with my friends, and that was that. I cooperated with them, I didn't hide the fact that I was getting booze or drugs from the men, but I didn't have any reason to trust them. We'd have our little chats, they'd hand me some leaflets about drugs or sexual health, and that would be that.

Why didn't they do anything? That was what I found most disturbing. If they had acted on what they knew and communicated between themselves I would have been spared massive abuse. But they didn't. The organisation that was meant to look out for me was in chaos – there were too many changes of staff and none of them kept good records, so the information just wasn't there. The people who were supposed to help me didn't seem to understand that something was dreadfully wrong. Even when they did recognise there was a problem, it seemed they put cost savings ahead of my welfare.

All these facts started to make sense now – the care system had failed to step in and help me when I needed it most. But it was more than that. There was an attitude about me. I felt it. I felt that the people involved in my life made assumptions about me and the choices I was making. That attitude prevented them from seeing the real issues. They thought: *she's going out all hours – that's her problem. If she's going to smoke and drink and take drugs, it's no wonder she's getting herself into mischief.* It felt like they were not on my side. Everyone was always reprimanding me and telling me off. The opinion among all the professionals – the social workers, teachers and police – was simply that I was naughty. I was going out all hours, not going to school, getting my dad into trouble. It was *my* fault, *my* attitude, *my* problem. To their minds I wasn't deserving of their help because I had made all the wrong choices. No wonder I felt that it was all my fault; everyone around me thought that too. And that attitude made it hard for me trust them enough to tell them what was going on. If somebody had said to me, 'These men are doing things to you that are not right, you're a child,' I might have reached out to them. But it wasn't like that. I was constantly in detention. I was arrested. I was told off. I was made to feel bad about myself.

My little boy Liam was born in February 2017, and though I was nervous about going through labour again, I had a better birth than with Elsa. He was born after twenty-two hours and this time I didn't need forceps, so his head was a normal shape. Once again, I fell completely and utterly in love. Liam was a lovely little thing with big blue eyes and dimples either side of his mouth. He took to the breast very well and Elsa was a devoted big sister from the word go. My life settled down into a happy routine of being a mum of two, and I loved it. I wanted to give them the childhood I never had, and I wanted them to experience all the things I longed for as a child. Taking them to the park, reading them bedtime stories, bath time, playing in the garden, painting at the kitchen table, dressing up, playdough . . . oh, there just weren't enough hours in the day! I felt I had so much love to pour into them, I could never give them enough.

'Another one?' Jake exclaimed, as I picked out the third bedtime story to read to Elsa as Liam nestled into my breast. 'You indulge them.'

'Oh, just one more won't hurt,' I laughed. 'This one is her favourite.'

Later, as I sat downstairs in the lounge, scrolling through all the hundreds of pictures I'd taken of the kids on my phone, trying to choose which ones to print off, I tried to explain how I felt to Jake.

'I've got no memories of anyone putting me to bed when I was little,' I said. 'I don't remember anyone reading me a bedtime story, pushing me on the swings, teaching me to ride a bike, playing with me. But that's what I wanted more than anything. So what if I read them an extra story at bedtime? Children just need your attention, that's all. They don't need fancy toys or expensive clothes. I know what a child needs and I just don't think it's possible to love them too much.'

My case against the council finally came before a mediator in November 2017 and Jake and I went up to London to negotiate the settlement. It was a very strange day – me and my solicitors were based in one room of a hotel while the council representatives were in another. Our lawyers assured me we had a strong case and that the council would prefer to go through mediation rather than having the trouble and expense of a lengthy trial, which they would almost certainly lose. To begin with they made a low offer of compensation but the barrister representing our case said it wasn't enough. All day long the mediator went back and forth between the rooms until, finally, he came back and said the council had made an offer for a full and final settlement of the case, which was more than double the original sum.

'They have categorically stated that they won't go any higher,' he said. My barrister said this was an acceptable figure, so we settled there.

It's something, I mused, as we took the train back down south from London and the urban sprawl gave way to open countryside. Jake put a hand on my knee and I put my hand over his. He smiled at me. *It is something – something to help me start my life again. Something to help put me back on track.* No amount of money would ever make up for the years of abuse I had suffered unnecessarily, or their failure to support me while my mother was ill, or to follow up the real physical abuse from my father. I had lost years of my life – I had lost my peace of mind, education, hopes for a future. But it was something. It was a start.

20.

A New Chapter

'LOOK, MUMMY!' ELSA HAULS a handful of grey, silty mud from the riverbed and her eyes nearly pop with excitement.

'That's great!' I laugh. 'Now bring it up to the mud kitchen and you can make something delicious with it.'

Elsa carefully carries her thick pile of mud up to the wooden shack near the river and instantly pretends to bustle about the kitchen in an almost-perfect imitation of me when I'm cooking.

'Now, let's make something tasty for tea, shall we, Liam?' she addresses her brother with a caring, maternal tone. 'What do you want to eat tonight? Shall I make shepherd's pie or lasagne?'

Liam perches on the little wooden stool next to his big sister and plunges his hands into the gooey mess.

'Not now, Liam, I'm making tea,' Elsa admonishes, and I can't help cracking up. It's uncanny – she has me down to a tee! It's July 2018 and we've gone away to our favourite camping spot in north Wales for a family holiday, along with Jake's two other children. I love camping. Just being outside, close to nature, in the fresh air all the time, makes me feel happy and relaxed. I love making packed lunches and taking the kids on long rambling walks through the Welsh hillsides, dotted with fluffy white sheep, even when it's cold and drizzly. Or waking up to the sound of bird song and snuggling tight in my sleeping bag, with one or both of the children trying to crawl in. At night we cook burgers and hot dogs on the barbeque and toast sweet marshmallows on the fire. Camping is a great way to get away from our daily lives. It means we all get to be together without the distraction of the TV or the many jobs we have at home. On holiday I'm a more relaxed version of me. I rarely get stressed out or upset. It's like a form of therapy.

All the kids get on well together and we have brought plenty of outdoor toys like the frisbee, cricket set and swing ball, so they can play all day long. Liam is too small to join in many of the games but, bless him, he tries. He's a really boyish boy – he loves to run around, climb trees, kick around a football and skateboard. It's funny watching him copy Jake's older boys – he never sees the danger or his own limitations. Of course, it's a nightmare being his mum – I have to watch him like a hawk – but I don't want to stop him trying. There's something wonderful in his adventurous spirit and his determination to do what the big boys do. There's only one rule: nobody plays beyond the windbreakers. That is my rule. You can play what you like, as long as you are playing where I can see you. I have to be able to see the kids at all times. The older boys complain but I refuse to compromise on this. And yes, perhaps I'm a stricter mother than most, perhaps I'm warier of strangers. Well, I've got good reason to be wary. I try not to let it get in the way of their lives – after all, I want them to have a normal childhood – but if Elsa is invited to a friend's birthday party I'm not the mum that drops her off at the door, only to pick her up two hours later. I'm there the whole time, watching her, making sure she's okay.

It is all I have ever wanted – a family of my own – and I try to be the best mother I can possibly be. I try to give them love, support and guidance because that's what I lacked when I was a child. I praise their drawings, telling them how good they are at art; I encourage their learning and help them to do their numbers. I want them to succeed where I failed. I want them to have a good education, the chance of a proper future – all the things I missed. They don't want for anything, certainly not the important stuff. I tell my kids I love them every day and they get tons of cuddles. I would give them hourly if I could! They have good routines for their health and hygiene, they eat proper home-cooked food and they know their manners. But, most importantly, I listen to them. I try to give them my full attention and make sure all their needs are met. And you know what, they are really happy, healthy children. Seeing how they're growing and developing, hitting all their milestones, makes me feel proud. It makes me feel I'm doing everything right. There is real love in our home – quite often my kids will come up to me and give me a little kiss or a cuddle, and that makes everything better. With their love I can deal with anything that life throws at me.

It saddens me that my mother never got to meet my kids because I know she would have loved them both and would have been so happy for me. It's a shame they don't have any family on my side. They have plenty on Jake's side, but they know nothing about my family in Halifax. I can't go back there ever again. My dad has made no effort to visit and I'm not sure he deserves to know the kids. My sisters don't come down to see me either. It's sad but I try not to think about it too much. Generally, Elsa and Liam are the source of all my happiness. They are truly the light in my life.

One thing is for sure – whatever my paternity, I'm certainly not my father's daughter. I'm a devoted, hard-working mum and I make sure that our home is as nice as it can possibly be. I spend a lot of time tidying, cleaning, decorating and generally thinking of ways to improve our environment. It is the home I dreamed of having when I was a child – warm, comfortable, welcoming and filled with delicious smells from home-cooked meals. Jake is appreciative of my efforts, though he occasionally tells me off for going over the top. He jokes that the kids get seventeen meals a day and that I have fallen in love with storage tidies. It's true – I can spend hours on the internet, looking at storage boxes! It makes us both laugh but I don't deny that I put a lot of energy and effort into keeping a nice home. The kids have slides and swings in the garden, there are numerous framed photos of the children on the walls and, if anything breaks, we fix it. See, Dad, it's not that difficult to make a nice home for your family. All it takes is effort. And I suppose that was the one thing you didn't want to spend on me.

The trauma is still there, still bubbling below the surface, and though I try not to let it interfere with my everyday life, there are times it overwhelms me. I know the fear may be irrational, but just being around an Asian man scares me, and the panic attacks come when I least expect them. Jake recently dropped me at Poundland to stock up on snacks for the kids. I was standing in the queue, laden down with crisps and biscuits, when I spotted that the cashier was a short Asian man with a goatee. *Oh no. No, no, no! He looks just like . . . just like . . .* my heart started to pound, my breathing became rapid and shallow and I could feel myself being pulled into the tight grip of a panic attack. Calm down, calm down, I told myself. It's nothing. He's not one of them. But the more I told myself to calm down, the worse I felt. I wanted to burst into tears and run away. *What can I do? What can I do?* Finally, Jake appeared at the entrance to the shop. I walked purposefully towards the exit, shoved the snacks in his hand, whispered 'please pay' and left. It took ages to feel normal again.

It isn't uncommon, I'm told, to suffer from ongoing trauma, considering the experiences I've been through. The consultant psychiatrist who assessed me for my case against the council diagnosed PTSD and said I will probably always suffer from social anxiety as well as trust issues. But in some ways, it has got worse over the years. I've always struggled with body confidence but since I had my children, I've found physical intimacy with Jake very hard. I feel self-conscious, unconfident, and I won't have sex unless it's in the dark. It's difficult for him and I don't know how to explain it to him. All I know is, it's taking a long time for me to come to terms with what happened. Perhaps it'll take many years – after all, for many years my body was abused and misused.

As the years go by, I feel more protective over my body, more and more sensitive about how I am touched.

The psychiatrist described me as 'socially avoidant', which means that I struggle to leave the house. I suppose that's true when it comes to crowded spaces like town centres or shopping malls. I am very self-conscious in social situations. I won't venture outside unless I'm wearing a full face of make-up and I worry that people 'know' about me, that they think I'm a 'tramp' or 'easy'. In my rational mind, I know this can't possibly be true, but it's a feeling that has worsened over the years. That is why the council had to pay out so much money – it's for the counselling I will need. The panic attacks, social avoidance, insecurity, I don't want to live with it forever and I certainly don't want it to hold me back for the rest of my life. I refuse to let my past determine my future.

After the case ended and I went back to 'normal' life, I felt sure that I would want to put everything behind me and move forward. But something felt unfinished. Everyone said I had got 'justice' but somehow it didn't feel like it. Yes, I had achieved the aim of putting the perpetrators behind bars and, in the very narrowest sense, 'criminal justice' had been achieved. But I felt something deeper was unfulfilled – my sense of natural justice had not been satisfied. Then, several weeks after the case ended, Anna came to tell me that she would no longer be able to act as my social worker. Thanks to her experience with my case, she had been offered a post heading up a new CSE unit, helping to raise awareness and bring about changes to the lives of girls who might be going through the same thing I did. I was sad to say goodbye, of course, but pleased for her – pleased too that her involvement with me had led her down an important new path in her life. She felt she could do a lot of good, using the knowledge she had gained from my case. And that got me thinking – maybe I could use my experiences for good too. Maybe I should also get involved in helping to raise awareness about CSE.

That was what led me to writing this book. Anna put me in touch with Hope Daniels, the author of *Hackney Child*. She too had been through a terrible childhood and had come out the other end and written a bestselling memoir about her experiences. Hope was amazing – she encouraged me to speak out, recommending an agent who teamed me up with ghostwriter Katy Weitz. Together, Katy and I set about putting my experiences down on paper. It hasn't been the easiest journey – as I said, I had looked forward to putting this part of my life behind me, so reliving some of the worst aspects of my story has been deeply distressing. But in a way I have found it easier than the police interviews because I know that this book is for me. This is *my* story, the way I want to tell it. The problem with going through a court case is that you only get to tell a small part of the story, the part that relates to the crime. You don't get to explain all the other stuff that comes before that, such as the reasons why I was out late at night at the age of eleven, the way I felt about my home life, the difficulties I faced as a young carer for my dying mum and the harsh reality of life with my dad – all the things that conspired to make me easy prey to the men who were out there.

I know a lot has changed in Halifax – health agencies are now trained in spotting the signs of CSE, there are better lines of communication between professionals, as well as training for taxi drivers and hoteliers and those within the Asian community to help identify girls at risk. There are more people looking out now – but that's not to say the danger is over. I know that for a fact because dozens of men who raped me never got caught. So they are still out there – and would they do it again? Almost certainly. So we have to educate everyone – parents, carers, teachers, neighbours, GPs, police and all those who come into contact with children. We have to talk to young girls about what CSE looks like, stop blaming them for just being naturally curious and experimental teenagers, and start trying to understand how a situation like this can take hold.

So that is what I plan to do with my future. I want to help open up the discussion about Child Sexual Exploitation so that, together, as a community, we can help prevent it happening again. And that, for me, is what justice feels like. That is what I plan to work on until I am no longer capable of working. And who knows when that will be. It's a funny thing, knowing that my life is going to be cut short by an inherited disease. In some ways, it feels very unfair. I get frustrated at the way others take it for granted that they will grow old in a fit, healthy body.

'When I retire, I'm going to go travelling round the world,' Jake says in a thoughtless moment and I think to myself, *Well, I won't be coming with you.* But I try not to let it get me down. I try to think of the now, I try to think of the joy I can take from this life today, and that is really all I can do. The long-term future is unclear for me. All I really have is now.

So Huntington's is good in some ways – I can live in the

moment easier than others who might be concerned for future or consumed by the past. I let all that go because, either way, I can't change it. Instead, I take joy from the small things in life – a quiet, peaceful bath, a sunny day at the park, the excitement of a special occasion like a birthday or Christmas when I spoil the children with presents. And I treasure the little moments that make up our daily lives, like the way Elsa giggles when I tickle her back at bedtime or the feeling of Liam's little body as he hugs my knees. Or even just sitting on the sofa at night with Jake, watching *Corrie*, holding hands. One day I'll have to face Huntington's but not today. Today I will try to live the best life I can. I have goals, I have hopes and I have dreams. But I try to hold them lightly, because, like a balloon, a sudden gust may suddenly blow them all away and I will have no control over that at all.

I know that one day I'll tell my children about what happened to me. And if I'm too ill, the book will tell them for me. Not too soon, though; not until they're old enough to understand and cope with the knowledge. I want them to stay innocent for as long as possible. I know I can't wrap them in cotton wool and I don't intend to. They must learn to be independent of me, because I know that they face a future without me in it. But I won't snatch their childhood away. Just being able to watch them enjoy the simple, innocent pleasures of playing together is enough to make me whole inside.

I am lucky. You may not think so, but I consider myself a lucky person.

I was given a second chance that saved my life. I hope my

story shows that no matter how bleak and hopeless you feel, it is possible to come out of a bad situation and start again. I felt trapped – but I wasn't. I escaped and I want to share that hopeful thought with everyone reading this. No matter how bad things seem, don't give up. Don't ever stop hoping. If I can do it, anyone can. And if I can wake up every day with a smile on my face, then you can too. Today, I know I am lucky to be alive. I am so grateful to Pete, Anna, Sheila and Adam – together they saved my life, put me back in one piece and set me on the right path. Now I want to reach out to families whose children might be victims of CSE and show them how to help them. Sometimes you just need time, patience and a whole lot of love. And never, never to forget that these are children, just children. I can't change what happened to me but I hope to change someone else's future. And put a little bit of love back into the world.

Acknowledgements

A huge and heartfelt thank you to my foster family for all their love, support and guidance.

Thanks to my social worker, Anna, for always being there for me.

Thank you to the police and all the professionals who worked on my case – I am grateful to you all for your incredible dedication, professionalism and expertise.

Thank you to Jake for being there through everything, for encouraging me and for giving me the strength and support to see the case through to the end. But, more than that, thank you for our two beautiful children.

Finally, thank you to Katy Weitz for helping me write my story.

Child Sexual Exploitation (CSE) – How to Spot the Signs

CHILD SEXUAL EXPLOITATION IS a complex form of abuse that can be difficult to identify and assess. It is impossible to say how many children are at risk in the UK today, though, according to BBC News, local authorities raised 18,800 concerns of children at risk across the UK in 2016–17. This was the equivalent of fifty-one every day. Many may have already experienced and suffered some form of abuse, whether that be neglect, physical, emotional or sexual. Children need help, but they may not know where to look and many do not recognise they are victims. Sometimes children are made to bring along other children for the abusers, or they may take other children along and are unaware of the risks they are exposing them to. Children need to be treated as victims and helped to break free from CSE. It is everyone's responsibility to safeguard children from CSE, and therefore important that everyone, from parents to carers, neighbours, shop workers, taxi drivers, hotel staff to professionals, knows how to spot the signs of CSE and what action to take.

Here, with the help of Cassie's former social worker, Anna, now working in the field of CSE, we answer some of the most pressing and practical questions surrounding the issue and address important areas like grooming, consent and building healthy relationships.

Q. What is Child Sexual Exploitation (CSE)?
A. The official government definition used today is this: 'Child Sexual Exploitation is a form of child sexual abuse. It occurs where an individual or group takes advantage of an imbalance of power to coerce, manipulate or deceive a child or young person under the age of eighteen into sexual activity either in exchange for something the victim needs or wants and/or for the financial advantage or increased status of the perpetrator or facilitator. The victim may have been sexually exploited even if the sexual activity appears consensual. Child Sexual Exploitation does not always involve physical contact; it can also occur through the use of technology'.

Q. What is grooming?
A. There are four stages of the grooming process – it is important that children, their carers and everyone else understands this process.

1. **Targeting** – Where a perpetrator will 'target' a child. They will find a place where children go e.g. shopping centre, park or online.

2. **Friendship/befriending** – The perpetrator will start talking to a child, building trust, getting to know them, making them

feel they are safe. They might offer a shoulder to cry on, support them, pay them compliments, give them time and attention or buy them gifts and take them places.

3. **Caring** – The perpetrator becomes more caring and builds on the befriending stage, making the child think they are the only person there for them. At this stage they start to isolate the child from safe people and they become more intense with the child.

4. **Abusive** – The perpetrator will change and become abusive, making the child carry out sexual acts either with them or with someone else.

It is important to note that a perpetrator can move between these stages. The length of time between each stage varies, as does the pattern.

Q. Who does it happen to?

A. Child Sexual Exploitation can happen to any child under the age of eighteen. Boys as well as girls. Children of all races and backgrounds. Those particularly at risk and vulnerable are children experiencing problems at home, those who go missing and children who are in care. It is important to note that CSE can also happen to those from a loving and supportive home.

It is never, ever a child's fault if they are affected by CSE, even if they agreed to the sexual activity because they felt they 'should'. A child may agree to sexual activity because they felt they had no other choice and/or do not fully understand consent.

Q. Who does it?

A. The media has placed huge emphasis on CSE being perpetrated by Asian men, however there is no standard profile of an exploiter – people who commit this crime can be male or female and come from all races or backgrounds. What they have in common is that they usually have something over the child they target. For example, they might be older, wealthier, physically stronger than them, or possess a status that makes them seem 'cool' to others. They might give support and attention that no one else provides. They may listen, offer advice or give compliments to the child. Perpetrators are becoming increasingly sophisticated, using the internet to protect their identity and trafficking (moving a person from one place to another for the purposes of CSE) children around the country to avoid detection.

There is no age restriction on the perpetrator – they can be under eighteen. With this in mind it means CSE can be hard to spot even for the child who is being exploited. A child can be groomed over time or it can happen very quickly, so they may not be aware they are a victim and many victims will be made to feel by the perpetrator that it is their fault.

Q. What are the signs/indicators of CSE?

A. It is not always easy to recognise the signs/indicators of CSE, however there are a number of indicators that you can look out for. This can be tricky as some of these could be present in a teenager's life who is not being exploited. However, put together – and with your own knowledge of the child at risk – some of these signs may be indicative of CSE:

- **Physical health:** bruising, love bites, cuts, scratches, grab marks, making disclosures of physical or sexual harm.
- **Sexual health:** sexually transmitted infections (STIs), recurring or multiple STIs, pregnancy, terminations, miscarriages, inconsistent stories, sexually risky behaviour.
- **Emotional health:** low self-esteem or confidence, crying, self-harm/overdose, eating disorders, depression, suicide attempts, volatile behaviours, violent or aggressive behaviour, secretive behaviour.
- **Education:** Poor attendance, truanting, going missing from school, refusal/disengagement with education.
- **Missing from home:** Returning late with no plausible explanation, going missing, coming and going at strange times, staying out overnight.
- **Social presentation:** Change in appearance e.g. dressing older, putting on more make-up, wearing clothing not bought by known person. Appearing to be intimidated or fearful of certain people, secretive behaviour, lack of interest in previous hobbies or activities.
- **Housing:** Being unhappy at home, pattern of street homelessness or unstable accommodation, having keys to premises other than those known about.
- **Income:** Possession of items with no plausible explanation e.g. mobile phone, clothes, cigarettes or alcohol. Social activities with no plausible explanation of how they have been funded.
- **Places:** Seen at public toilets known for cottaging or adult venues (pubs, clubs, saunas), reports that a young person has

been seen in CSE hotspots or areas of concern, getting in/out of cars with unknown adults.
- **Relationships:** Associating with other young people at risk or involved in CSE, unexplained sexual involvement with an older person, inappropriate or increased use of the internet or mobile phones, contact with known or suspected inappropriate adults or gang activity.
- **Other:** Reports from reliable sources suggesting child is at risk of sexual exploitation, youth offending behaviour, known or suspected of being at risk from gangs or trafficking.

Some or all of the above may be present to help you spot CSE. However, it is also important to recognise that there may only be one sign/indicator which, when explored, leads to finding out further information, which indicates a risk of CSE and in exceptional cases there may be no indicators.

Q. Why don't children disclose CSE?
A. There may be many reasons why children do not feel able to disclose CSE, some of them are listed below:
- Not recognising they are being exploited – caught in the grooming process.
- Shame/embarrassment/guilt.
- Fear of perpetrator – they will have made threats to harm them and their family/friends.
- Silenced by perpetrator/not knowing how to say the words and explain what is happening/they have never been asked and are waiting for this.

- Attachment or loyalty to the perpetrator.
- Self-blame – they feel responsible for the abuse as the perpetrator tells them this.
- Fear of not being believed – perpetrators will have told them this.
- Fear of causing family problems if parents/carers know.
- Fear of professionals.
- Cultural taboos/feeling family shame.
- Not having anyone to talk to.
- Confusion/fear over sexuality/sexual identity if perpetrator is same sex as them.

Q. Why do children return to their abusers?
A. People may ask why children return to their abusers and there are many reasons for this. Many victims of CSE are unaware they are victims; they may feel they are getting their needs met in some way and may be fearful of the perpetrator. They may be receiving threats of harm to them or their family and feel obliged to continue the contact.

According to psychotherapist Zoe Lodrick, they may be suffering from Trauma Bonding – Trauma Bonding is loyalty to a person who is abusive. It is an unhealthy and unsafe attachment. Manipulation is always involved in creating this attachment. Often those experiencing Trauma Bonding are 'looking right at it but can't see it'. Children do not recognise they have been groomed and exploited and it becomes very hard for them to break free.

Even when a child does try to stay away, perpetrators will often make many attempts to seek them out. They could linger in places the child goes or make contact via phone. It is therefore important children have a wrap-around support package to safeguard them from CSE.

Q. If I have concerns as a parent, how do I approach my child about the subject of CSE?

A. Be aware of the signs of CSE and trust your gut feelings. Some of the things you might be questioning are: Have they been excessive with their phone? Are they getting a lot of texts or phone calls? Are they staying out late or coming home at strange times? Are they in possession of gifts or items they didn't previously own? Have they isolated themselves from others?

Continue to build a positive relationship with your child, encouraging open and honest conversations about everyday life and matters that are affecting them. Be ready to have conversations about CSE. Think about the venue and atmosphere and talk to them sensitively during an activity such as in the car, sat in the bedroom, or while making dinner or getting ready for bed. In a caring and curious manner ask them questions, consider your tone and approach, for example: 'I'm just curious, where did you get that alcohol/phone/money you had the other night?' or 'Where have you been going when you're not at home or returning back late?' Try not to approach your child in a confrontational or angry manner i.e. shouting or sitting them down to make accusations.

Be mindful that if your child is being groomed, they may not be honest in the answers they give you – they are likely to be very scared and you need to support them to feel safe. Be mindful of their body language and again trust your instincts, as you know your child better than anyone. Some parents/carers may not feel confident to have such discussions with their child if they are worried. If this is the case, then please share your concerns with a professional who will be able to help you. If you suspect your child is at risk of CSE then please seek immediate help from a professional such as the police or the Children's Social Care department of your local council.

Q. How do we stop a child becoming a victim of CSE to begin with?

A. Giving children education around grooming/CSE/consent/relationships/risks dangers etc. is the key to prevention. It is important to start conversations with children at a young age and help them to understand what is safe and not safe. You could talk to your children in an age appropriate way about sexual abuse. For example, the underwear rule: 'These body parts under your swimwear are yours, nobody is to touch them or want to look at them unless you are hurt, and a doctor may need to do this.' The education is about giving children this information to help them keep themselves safe, know the difference between right and wrong, and enable them to tell someone if they are feeling unsafe. Later, as they get older, they may have their own phone and access to social media e.g. Snapchat. Give them information about the dangers of people pretending to be nice online and talk to them about the grooming process and CSE. Armed with that information, they will be better able to spot the warning signs themselves.

Protecting children from CSE is also about ensuring their needs are met. Children whose needs are not met may be susceptible to a perpetrator. Giving children positive activities and opportunities will help; find local clubs, hobbies, sports etc. This will keep children engaged, help them to make friends, build confidence and resilience and minimise the opportunity for somebody to target the child.

Parental supervision is important too – children growing up will have time away from their parents/carers, therefore it is important that you carry out checks such as knowing your child's friends and their parents, knowing where your child is, who they are with and where they are going, and giving them appropriate curfew times. This is similar for a child's phone and social media use. Of course, none of this is fool proof, as a child could be approached on Facebook while they are at home, under parental supervision, and they might be encouraged to send indecent images.

The early identification of CSE and preventative action is the most effect way to tackle CSE.

Q. What is consent?
A. The Sexual Offences Act 2003 says 'a person has consented if he/she agrees by choice and has the freedom and capacity to make that choice. Choice is defined as a deliberate and active decision. Freedom is without power imbalance, manipulation, exploitation or duress and free from threats/force – even subtle.'

The law says you have to be sixteen or over to engage in sexual activity. Consent means two people saying yes. They can say no. They can say yes then change their mind. Sometimes they feel they have to engage due to fear etc.; this is not consent. If they are under the influence of drugs or alcohol, this is not consent.

Q. What is a healthy/unhealthy relationship?
A. All relationships go through good and bad patches but, on the whole, your relationships should leave you feeling safe, respected and liked for who you really are. According to CSE The Signs, there are signs you can look for to tell you whether yours is a healthy relationship.

FIVE SIGNS OF A HEALTHY RELATIONSHIP
1. You talk and listen to one another – Being able to talk often and openly is one of the most important parts of any relationship. So too is being genuinely interested in the other person's life and listening when they are the one doing the talking.

3. You trust each other – You trust each other to be honest, to mean what you say and to do what you say you'll do. You don't worry that you're being told half-truths or lies, or ever have reason to feel unsafe.

4. You feel respected – You feel like your opinion matters. You might still disagree from time to time, but you can talk calmly and honestly about how you are feeling. When you care about one another, you want each other to be happy so you'll work out a solution between you.

5. You support one another – Life is a mix of up and downs. In a normal relationship you'll feel supported at all times. You'll celebrate together when something really good happens to one or both of you, and you'll offer each other a shoulder to cry on if you're sad or upset.

6. You have an equal say in things – The best relationships are those in which both people have an equal say, whether it's what you want to do or where you want to go. It shouldn't ever feel like a power struggle or that one person is getting their own way all the time.

SEVEN SIGNS OF AN UNHEALTHY RELATIONSHIP

Even the best relationships aren't easy all the time, but there are certain tell-tale signs that a relationship isn't normal – or worse, that it's abusive. While you might be tempted to put someone's behaviour down to them having an off day, you should never put up with a bad or abusive relationship. It can destroy your self-confidence, cut you off from your friends and family, and even put your life at risk. Here are CSE The Signs' seven indicators of an unhealthy relationship.

1. **Emotional** – You're criticised or made to feel stupid. The decisions you make are controlled by the other person: from where you go and what you wear, to how you spend your money.

2. **Physical** – You're physically hit, kicked, slapped or punched – whether it's a one-off incident or on a regular basis.

3. **Sexual** – You're forced to do something sexual that you don't want to do, either for your friend, boyfriend or girlfriend, or for one or more of their friends.

4. **Intimidation** – You feel afraid of the other person because of the nasty things they say to you or message you.

5. **Manipulation** – You're made to feel guilty or jealous so that you'll do things you don't really want to do. Or you might be given gifts then be expected to do something in return.

6. **Isolation** – You're allowed to see and speak to your friends or family less and less. Sometimes not at all.

7. **Lack of communication** – Your friend, boyfriend or girlfriend keeps secrets from you or won't talk to you about things that are going on. Things that might be worrying or upsetting you.

Q. What can I do if I suspect a child/ young person I know is a victim of CSE?

A. Today, in many authorities, there is a specialist multi-agency CSE team that usually includes police, social workers, support workers, health professionals, schools, mental health, drug and alcohol advice workers and many more services. If you have concerns, the advice is to report this immediately to the police, children's social care, and your local CSE Team.

Some families can be afraid of reporting CSE; they may not want to involve the police or children's social care and may be worried their child is going to be removed – this is not the case. Social workers are there to help keep families together and safeguard children from CSE. It would be usual practice for the child and family to be visited by a social worker, police officer or both jointly. Do not feel worried about this, as they are trained to respond to CSE and support and safeguard the child and the family.

There are other professionals that you can tell such as those at school, a youth worker, GP or anyone who works with children in a professional capacity. All professionals are now well aware of and trained in CSE, they would not turn you away, and they will help and support the child and family. Police and partner agencies will work hard to tackle the perpetrator effectively and bring justice.

The important part is working in partnership with the child, the family and the professionals to safeguard from CSE. A plan will be put in place so everyone is working together. The overall aim is to safeguard the child and prosecute anyone committing CSE against children.

If you are a child and you are afraid this is happening to you or a friend or someone you know, then tell your parents/carers, an adult you trust and a professional. You will be helped and kept safe.

Q. What important messages can people think about?
A. Building a positive relationship with children is important when it comes to CSE – always be there for them, remain calm and patient, listen to them and help keep them safe. Make sure the child has supportive networks around them, so they always have someone they can talk to and there are always safe places for them

to go, away from their abusers. Build positive experiences for the child, ensuring they are in school or college, that they have clubs or hobbies that will keep them engaged, build their confidence and self-esteem and keep them away from their abusers. Police and Children's Social Care will always intervene to disrupt the CSE and safeguard the child and help the whole family.

FURTHER INFORMATION, HELP AND ADVICE

Childline
For help and advice on a wide range of issues, including help on supporting a friend. Free private and confidential helpline: 0800 1111 and private and confidential email through their website: www.childline.org.uk

PACE – Parents Against Child Exploitation
Leading national charity working with parents and carers of sexually exploited children, providing help, advice and support to all those involved. Lots of information and advice on safeguarding for parents, professionals and children.
https://paceuk.info/

Know about CSE
Helping to identify the signs of abuse.
http://knowaboutcse.co.uk/

NSPCC

The National Society for the Prevention of Cruelty to Children provides information, advice and a free, confidential helpline for anyone worried about any child. The 24/7 free, confidential helpline is 0808 800 5000 or you can email: help@nspcc.org.uk www.nspcc.org.uk

CSE The Signs

For parents/carers or children in need of advice about CSE/relationships/consent. http://csethesigns.scot